OUT OF
DARKNESS
INTO
THE LIGHT

OTHER BOOKS BY GERALD G. JAMPOLSKY, M.D.

To Give Is To Receive:
An 18 Day
Course On Healing Relationships

Love Is Letting Go Of Fear

Teach Only Love

Goodbye To Guilt

OUT OF DARKNESS INTO THE LIGHT

A Journey of Inner Healing

Gerald G. Jampolsky, M.D.

BANTAM BOOKS
NEW YORK · TORONTO · LONDON · SYDNEY · AUCKLAND

OUT OF DARKNESS INTO THE LIGHT

A Bantam Book / April 1989

Bantam trade edition / March 1990

Grateful acknowledgment is made for permission to reprint the following:
Portions reprinted by permission from A COURSE IN MIRACLES.
Copyright © 1975 Foundation for Inner Peace, Inc. Lyrics to
"Manuel Garcia" copyright © 1987 David Roth.

Library of Congress Cataloging-in-Publication Data

Jampolsky, Gerald G.
    Out of darkness into the light / Gerald G. Jampolsky.
        p.   cm.
    ISBN 0-553-34791-8
    1. Jampolsky, Gerald G.   2. Religious biography—United
States.   3. Physicians—United States—Biography.   4. Spiritual
life.   I. Title.
BL73.J36A3   1989
291.4—dc19
                                                          88-32084
                                                              CIP

Published simultaneously in the United States and Canada

PRINTED IN THE UNITED STATES OF AMERICA

OPM   18   17   16   15   14   13   12   11

CONTENTS

ACKNOWLEDGMENTS

I wish to express my heartfelt thanks to Diane Victoria Cirincione, whose consistent encouragement, patience, and love made this book possible. I would also like to give special thanks to Hal Zina Bennett for the many hours he spent with me in editing this book.

I am very grateful to Judith Skutch Whitson and Robert Skutch of The Foundation for Inner Peace for their permission to quote from *A Course in Miracles*. And I wish to express my deepest gratitude to the staff and the many people who have come to the Center for Attitudinal Healing, in Tiburon, California, and who have taught me the true meaning of trust, surrender, love, and peace.

Throughout the book you will find prayers, meditations, and prose poems. For the most part these are from my own writings. When they are from other sources, such as *A Course in Miracles*, they are noted as such.

OUT OF
DARKNESS
INTO
THE LIGHT

THE PASSING OF A DREAM

Help me out of my prison of darkness
Created by the shadows of my ego.
Awaken me from my dream of fear
Where guilt, blame, and attack
Beckon from shadowed doors.

Help me to see the world differently
By finding no value in blame
And self-condemnation.
Help me to experience Love
As my only reality.

Help me to cross only
The bridges of forgiveness
That I may come
Out of darkness
Into the Light.

Not so long ago, a book about a person's "fight with God" would have been the last thing in the world I would have wanted to read. The idea that I might write such a book would have been preposterous. *God* was a negative word for me. Besides, how can you fight with God?—since I had convinced myself that there just wasn't such an entity.

At the age of sixty-three, I now realize that, without having been aware of it, I was fighting with God most of my life. This may sound strange coming from a person who once proudly called himself an atheist—even more, a militant atheist—and did so in quite a superior manner.

I was sure that anyone who believed in God was intellectually soft, not tuned in to the "real" world. My snobbery was built on mountains of misguided thoughts. If anyone tried to strike up a conversation about God with me, I simply turned my back on them. I would have none of it.

And yet, my life had not always been like that. I can recall moments when I felt very different, when God seemed close enough to reach out and touch.

3

When I was about four years old, I was playing alone behind the apartment where we lived. The memory is crystal clear to me. It was one of the happiest moments of my childhood. I found myself talking to the daisies and the butterflies. And they were talking back. We carried on lengthy conversations. I remember feeling boundless love from them, and I recall how open and flowing my heart felt as I extended my love to them.

As a young child I also had conversations with the sky, the clouds, and with God. The joy I experienced during those moments was like beautiful music. I felt so *at one* with everything, and everything seemed so beautiful and so *forever*.

Whenever these memories threatened to surface in my adult life, I did my best to push them back. I held on to my militant atheist stand, maintaining my belief that people who were religious, who were on a spiritual journey—people who believed in God—were only victims of their own fears. In my mind the World War I statement that "there are no atheists in foxholes" was only further confirmation that people believed in God only when they were scared to death!

I believed that when you were fearful, you did not use your head. Fear made you intellectually soft. I was convinced that no definition of God could ever satisfy a person who was intellectually aware and alive. It never occurred to me, even for a second, that I might be the one who was fearful.

As a child I believed there was an external, superhuman God beyond the sky. I pictured him as an old man with a white robe, a long white beard, and bushy white eyebrows. I believed that if you did what God wanted you to do, you would be rewarded. If you went against God, you would be severely punished in some way. Mine was a belief in a frightening, vengeful, unforgiving God.

Only recently have I found that I am responsible for and can choose the thoughts I put into my mind. I know that only my thoughts can imprison me, and only my thoughts can set me free. It had never before occurred to me that in making decisions I have a choice between listening to my ego, with its voice of fear, or listening to the voice of God, the voice based on love. It is only of late that statements such as "Let my will and your will be one" or "Let thy will be done" have begun to ring true in my heart.

Immortality and Fear

Like my parents, I had always been fearful of death, since I thought my reality was limited to my body and my ego. This meant to me that when you died, that was the end, there was no more of anything. I decided that if that was the script God wrote, I wanted no part of it. At the same time I thought that people who talked about eternal life were dreamers who obviously did not know the facts.

What little faith I had in God disappeared when, at the age of sixteen, a good friend of mine was killed in an automobile accident. In my eyes, my friend's death was cruel, unfair, and insane. I was certain that there could not be a just, trusting, loving God. And that left me feeling more fearful, vulnerable, and unlovable than ever. Thereafter, I vacillated between believing there was no God and believing that God was surely out to get me.

I wanted my body to live forever. I fantasized about having my body frozen after death because maybe, just maybe, someone would discover a miracle drug that would bring me back to life and allow me to live forever. Before I was on a spiritual pathway, I saw death as the ultimate experience of the loss of control, and I sought to displace my fear of that by trying to control other people and the circumstances around me.

In spite of the external successes I had in my life, I always had a haunting feeling about the futility of life. That feeling was the voice of my ego, but I did not know that at the time. I felt there had to be more to life than I was experiencing. I thought there was no way on earth that I could continually protect myself from hurt or attack, from physical or emotional pain or illness. The bottom line for me in almost everything I did was my awareness of the impossibility of controlling death.

Whatever my ego said always felt like the truth to me. But now, finally, I see that the pictures my ego offers are only false images of the world and my place in it. My ego would have me believe that I am nothing more than a personality contained in a body that is limited to a particular time and space.

What Is the Ego?

I use the term *ego* in a different way than do most psychoanalysts. I view the ego as a false image, a form that is associated with the body and the physical self. It is a dream that denies our true identity as a spiritual self, a self that has no physical form.

The ego itself defies definition, but its effects on our lives are easy to discuss. The ego's main message is fear—fear that we are all alone in a world of scarcity and that we must seek (but never find) what we are looking for. It does not know the meaning of love and it sees peace as its enemy. It sees the world as a place of separation, of separate bodies and separate minds. It does not believe in wholeness or oneness. It would have us believe that our world is based far more on fear and attack than on love. It denies the existence of the spiritual self and tells us that reality is what we perceive through our physical senses. This book is about my struggle with the ego and my attempts to awaken to the spiritual self—the self that is not limited to a body or to time or space.

My battle with God was based on my ego's insistence that I believe in fear rather than in God; that I follow its dictates rather than let God be my director and my guide. Out of fear I attempted to rely—with little success—on my own plan, my own intellect, my own will, my own judgments, and my own past experiences. This, of course, is exactly what the ego wants us all to do.

I fought with God every time I allowed myself to block out my remembrance of God. So, every time I blamed another person or condemned myself, made a judgment, or became angry, on some level of my consciousness I was fighting with God.

I am now aware that I spent most of my life attempting to protect myself from what my ego perceived as attacks from others. I wore many disguises to hide my fears and true feelings from others—as well as from myself.

I used denial and repression to hide the truth from myself. My ego kept things hidden away in separate rooms in my mind, and sealed each room with steel doors so that there could be no communication between them. And even when I was screaming in terror in one of those rooms, no one could hear my screams.

My chaotic ego kept my adrenaline high, a condition from which I perceived the world as always on the offensive, always on the attack. It is no wonder that my posture in life became one of constant defensiveness.

Like a self-created god, I lived as though I had been put into this world to judge, change, control, and manipulate others. I attempted to fit them into molds of my own design, and in a most arrogant way I decided who was and who wasn't worthy of my attention.

Almost every day of my life was filled with fears created by my ego, warning me of all the awful things that were likely to happen to me. I was preoccupied with the pain I might suffer in the future. My decisions were self-centered and were based on what I thought would give me the most pleasure and the least pain, and without realizing it I often ended up confusing the two.

I was convinced that my miserable past was a forecast of a horrendous future, and of course I continued to act in ways that proved me right.

I always found it difficult to make decisions. I was obsessed with the idea that I would always make the wrong choice. The result was that I carried a huge burden of guilt on my shoulders. It is no small wonder, then, that most of my life I have been troubled with back pain.

I mistakenly thought that any love I received would be conditional, measured out to me on the basis of how well I performed or how much I produced. Moreover, I believed that my success could be measured by the quantity and quality of material possessions I acquired. I had yet to learn that I could never be truly happy if I was spiritually empty, focused on *getting* rather than *giving*.

There were times when I thought that life was filled with nothing but trials, and I did my best to hold on by the tips of my fingers. I was convinced that I had "to do this all by myself."

I discovered the hard way that decisions based on satisfying the ego do not bring happiness, peace, love, or fulfillment. On the contrary, they bring sadness, disappointment, darkness, conflict, and emptiness.

In 1973 my marriage of twenty years—a marriage that had produced two sons—ended in divorce. I became bitter and depressed. My guilt was overwhelming. I felt as though I was on an elevator plunging out of control to the ground. Life no longer seemed worth living. I turned more and more to alcohol, hell-bent on destroying myself.

I tried all kinds of conventional and unconventional therapies. Nothing helped. I was stopped for drunk driving more than once and was in danger of losing both my driver's and medical licenses. I was weary with fear and misery. The last thing in the world that interested me was God.

And then a miracle occurred. Until then the word *miracle* wasn't even in my vocabulary. In May 1975, Judy Skutch Whitson, a close and dear friend, called me from New York City. She was very excited about a manuscript she had just come across that she thought could change my life. "It's about God and spiritual transformation," she said. I was not in the least bit interested.

A few days later, Judy brought the manuscript to my home in California. It was entitled *A Course in Miracles*. I didn't even like the name. Judy persisted, urging me to examine the writing. I answered in a very condescending way, "All right, I'll read one page, but that is all."

What followed was an experience I have never been able to share fully, although I have tried to do so literally thousands of times. After reading that single page, I began to cry. Deep inside me a tiny voice said, "Physician, heal thyself. This is your way home."

I can only hint at what happened after that. I felt that the universe opened up to me, and I became part of everything that was. There was no separation, and I felt clear in the belief that the essence of my being was love. I felt a sense of peace and joy beyond anything I had ever before experienced.

In the depth of my soul I also had feelings of tenderness, softness, safety, and an inner knowledge that I was in God's presence. All of this had a timelessness about it. I felt that from that moment on, my whole life would be changed. I was going to live a life devoted to

God. In that one instant, I somehow knew that my life would be dedicated to giving.

I had never really understood what a mystical experience was, but I sensed that that was what I was experiencing. In my heart, I felt that a map of life was being given to me, and that God's will and my will would become one.

Looking back, it became clear that up until that moment I had been struggling with whose script I would follow in life—God's or my ego's. It also became clear that mine had been a solitary battle all along because God had never been engaged in it. I had been doing battle only with myself. I now feel that God was patiently waiting for me to let go of my false beliefs and come home to the Source of all Life, which I had never really left.

Through my study of *A Course in Miracles* I began to realize that there are only two ways to make decisions. The first one was already familiar to me: my old way of listening to the ego, a voice based on fear and separation. The second was the one I had just begun to learn, which was to listen to the voice of God, a voice based on love and joining.

Before this time, if anyone had told me it was possible to make decisions by letting God be the director, by choosing to let my will and God's will be one, I would have considered them crazy.

I now realize that I had been seeking all my life, but did not really know what I was looking for. Moreover, I now realize that all of humankind are seekers looking for the truth. We are all seeking to discover the eternal, and to fill the empty void of separation and loneliness that we have falsely created for ourselves.

Nothing had quenched the thirst of my desires on the physical plane. It had never occurred to me that I was seeking the wrong goal, or that I was searching in the wrong places. How clever the ego is in hiding the truth from our awareness! The complexity of my fear had kept me in darkness and blinded me to the simplicity of the final answer—that all I had to do was let go of my attachments to the outer world, and trust going inside.

The Ego Strikes Back

I have found, as I walk and sometimes stumble on my way home to God, that I have a very stubborn ego. It doesn't want to give up and vanish without a fight. Frequently when I am in conflict, I find that I have chosen to have that conflict by letting my ego take command. When this happens there is usually something in my outer world that I feel I must have. Each time I let go of one such desire, it seems to be replaced with another.

I continue to find it difficult to distinguish between the voice of my ego and the voice of God. I am certainly no expert at listening to my inner voice, my inner teacher. More often than not I am confused about which voice it is that I am responding to.

When I am feeling the most sane, there is one thing about which I am always certain: my intention to open up my heart to God. It is then that I want to turn all my problems over to God and to go in the direction of love and peace.

I have also discovered that my ego looks upon peace of mind as a great enemy. The moment I am at peace, my ego produces a million temptations to interrupt that peace because of the ego's desire to get rid of it.

It really doesn't take much for me to be attracted to guilt and suffering. It is almost as if I offer my guilt button to anyone who will push it. Wherever I am, I don't have much trouble finding that person.

In the flash of a second, my ego puts up a radar antenna; and I, suddenly motivated by fear and separation, begin to judge the motives and behavior of people around me. I then become filled with doubt, distrust, fear, anger, and conflict.

I feel most sane when I have no attachments to anything and I remember that I really don't know what is best for other people or myself. It is then that I enjoy my greatest success with hearing my inner voice.

I hear my inner teacher when I still my mind, when I let go of my past and my ego and come to God with empty hands. That is the time I experience the greatest inner peace.

At times I feel that the closer I get to the Light, the more dark nights of the soul I experience. My ego continues to be quite feisty, but I am learning how to take responsibility for that feistiness. Although most of the time I think I'd rather be happy than right, I am still amazed at how often my ego takes over and I choose to be right, at the expense of my happiness and that of those people around me.

More and more, as I retrain my mind, I am impressed with the magnitude of my ego's deceptiveness, ambiguity, and ambivalence, and how frequently I have put myself and others in "lose-lose" situations. And I am learning that when I am angry at my ego, things just get worse.

I am learning to be quiet when in distress, to be polite to my ego, to see no value in its chatter. My ego becomes quiet when I choose to live one second at a time, and to use that time to help and love rather than to judge.

Surrendering to Love

Since 1975 I have been making a conscious effort to put an end to my self-made fight with God by surrendering to love. The surrender is not easy since it requires letting go of the ego-self and no longer finding value in fear and separation. This book is about that fight and my continuing efforts to surrender, to leave the ego behind, and to come out of the darkness into the Light.

At times I have awakened in the middle of the night and words have poured from me, reminding me of the magnificent beauty, joy, peace, and safety that we can all experience by accepting God's unconditional love. At other times I have awakened to the terror and cries of my ego, and words from my insane mental state have flowed from me. Some of these have taken the form of poems.

Until recently I kept these poems private, using them only to increase my own awareness. When I was writing them I had no intention of publishing them.

There was a part of me that felt embarrassed by what I thought was a childlike, mushy, intimate quality to some of my writings. Yet, as I began sharing them in my lectures, I found that others felt and experienced the very same things I was describing, people who were struggling through their own dark nights of the soul. I have found that these personal writings can give strength, courage, and hope to others on spiritual paths, so I offer them to you in this book.

Although sometimes I still fight with God, I feel that God's Light is becoming brighter and more consistent in my life, leading me out of the darkness of my ego and into the Light of God's love.

The seconds of stillness and love have increased, seconds when I can fully accept and trust that God loves me totally, perfectly, completely, and eternally. I am beginning to see that I don't have to judge or interpret the motives and behavior of others. There is no need to decide who are the good guys and who are the bad, who should be blamed and who punished. I find it truly is "safe" to surrender the script written by me and trust in God's script.

I find peace when I have forgiveness in my heart. I find it when I am helpful to others, and I find it when I choose to see innocence in everyone, including myself.

With all of my heart, my hope is that you, the reader, may benefit from my writings and reflections, finding strength, comfort, and faith from the stories I tell of the many people who have been my teachers.

I now have hope. And if there is hope for one like me, who thought he was beyond all help and who believed he had more guilt, shame, and inadequacy than anyone else in the world, then rest assured that there is hope for you.

—Gerald G. Jampolsky, M.D.
Tiburon, California
December 1987

1

A MAP OF LIFE

What is this cancer inside me?
The fiery anger that lingers,
In its thin disguise . . .
The coldness and the brittleness
That comes from my pores
At a moment's notice.

Could it all be fear,
And nothing but fear?
Is there no roadmap
That can lead me to peace
And freedom?

Can I really feel
Whole and at one
By simply crossing
The bridge of forgiveness?

Why does something
That seems so simple
Bring out my greatest
Resistance?

Obstacles, obstacles, obstacles.
Is that all there is to life—
A series of obstacles
Separating me from others?

When will I awaken to
The full awareness
That all obstacles
Between myself and others
Are self-imposed?

I have manufactured them
Through my own fear of love
And my own fear of God.

No one ever gave me a roadmap for how to be happy in life. I never received a map for being a happy child, or for being an adolescent who was not in conflict, or for being a peaceful adult, or for being a successful parent, or for growing old gracefully. Whatever roadsigns I saw seemed to indicate conflicting directions.

If there is a recurrent theme in my life, it is that I thought I was going somewhere, only to travel a long way and end up exactly where I started. I know that I am not alone in this: many have had similar experiences in their lives. For me, the same frustrations kept reappearing. Fear, stress, unhappiness, and feeling unloved were my constant companions.

It is as if the ego keeps telling us that we must search in life but never find what we are seeking. For me, breaking habits and old behavior patterns seemed almost impossible. Life was filled more with despair than fun. And try as I might, I could not find the way to free myself from going around in circles. I had no roadmap for happiness.

But the truth is that even if we were presented with the best roadmap in the world, it would be useless unless we had a clear sense of where we are now and where we want to go. For the roadmap to be effective we must have a concept of who and what we truly are. We must know the purpose of our life's journey and believe in it.

These are concepts that I, like so many others, took for granted most of my life, never questioning very deeply, never looking closely at what I needed to do to give my life coherence. Caught up in my fragmented and sometimes chaotic life, I often did not find the time to look at these concepts with any depth and clarity.

Regardless of how it looked to the outside world, I never felt that my goals were consistent. I think I share a common experience with a great many people, a feeling of being lost but not wanting to admit it to myself or to others. So many of us feel that we are like the proverbial little lambs who have lost their way. We feel like strangers in the world, never quite sure where to find our real homes.

To start a journey, we need to be certain of our identities, to know who and what we are. Before I found a path of spiritual guidance, I felt that my entire identity consisted of my ego, the person in this body named Jerry Jampolsky. I felt that I was the sum total of what I did in life and there really wasn't any more to life than that. Being a physician was part of my identity. Another part was my belief that my body was here for only a limited time. Sooner or later I would die, and that would be the end of my life and the end of my identity. Because there were so many people around me who shared that belief, I never saw any reason to question it.

Over the years it has been pointed out to me that we limit ourselves and others when we create labels for one another, categorizing ourselves by the work we do. In the past, after being with a person less than two minutes, I would ask, "What do you do?" When they answered "doctor," "bus driver," "teacher," etc., I would judge their value and determine whether I wished to spend more time with them.

The possibility that our true identities could be found in our spiritual beings, or that what we are is love, and that our true reality might have nothing to do with our vocations, bodies, or egos, had previously seemed both preposterous and illogical to me.

In 1974 I had an experience that taught me that there might be another way to relate to others and to myself. I was at a cocktail party. Not in the mood for small talk, I saw an empty couch and headed toward it. Just as I sat down, another man took a seat beside me.

We immediately struck up a conversation and had a wonderful time. We talked from our hearts about many things, and we spoke in depth. Time seemed to fly. Later, our hostess joined us. "I'm so glad you two met," she said. "I can see from your animated conversation how much you enjoy each other." We agreed.

The man and I had never introduced ourselves. It turned out that he was a world-renowned concert pianist. When our hostess told him I was a psychiatrist, he laughed and said, "I hate psychiatrists. If you had introduced yourself as one, I probably would have walked away."

I laughed. Then it was my turn to confess: "If I'd known you were a famous musician, I would have felt so inadequate and threatened I couldn't have talked to you, either."

Perhaps our identities have more to do with our hearts than with what we do with our bodies in our day-to-day lives.

Early Roadmaps

We learn and accept much about our identities through our parents, of course. However, a great part of our identities is focused on the creation of the ego's road-map for life. By looking back at my earliest experiences, I find that I become better acquainted with my ego and begin to recognize its voice in my present life. I then start seeing my ego a little more clearly and can recognize its voice of fear and separation when it shouts at me.

One very loud part of its voice is in my parents' philosophy that yesterday was awful, today is horrendous, and tomorrow will be even worse, so one must be on guard at all times. Listening to the voice of that belief system led me to depression and hopelessness. I learned a lot about this part of my roadmap from my mother, who was a very protective person.

Sometimes I would get split messages from my parents. For example, on one Sunday drive we came to a very steep hill that my mother said was too dangerous to drive up. She had my father stop at the bottom so that she could get out and walk up the hill; she got back into the car at the top. It did not occur to me until years later that in spite of how dangerous it was in her mind, my mother had allowed the rest of us to drive up that hill.

Another thing I remember is that my parents were always telling me to hurry. It didn't matter what I was doing—getting dressed, taking a bath, eating, going off to school—I was never fast enough. I especially remember dinners with my family. With five of us at the table, everything was done in a great rush. Dishes were passed quickly, food was scooped out in a flash, and we all ate as fast as we could. It was partly from this experience that I integrated the "hurry concept" into the other aspects of my roadmap. I ran through each day at full speed, never quite sure if I was running away from something or toward it, and never certain why I was in such a hurry. My ego drove me to rush, although it seldom came up with any good reasons for doing so.

As a child I was always fidgeting, always in motion—in today's terms, I would have been labeled *hyperkinetic* or *hyperactive*—and if there was a choice of directions to take, I invariably chose the wrong one. Looking back, I have the impression that I was always spilling milk and bumping into things. From all this I picked up another aspect of my roadmap—an impression of myself as a clumsy clod, which my ego-self was only too willing to adopt.

I always left a big dust storm behind me and must have driven my poor parents to distraction. I never walked if I could run, and I continued to bump into things and lose my way. My frenetic energy was very difficult for most people around me.

❦

Both of my parents were immigrants. They lived their lives pretty much as their parents had done, working extremely hard and worrying most of the time. Their personal identities were centered on sacrificing almost everything for their children. Today I would describe them as having been devoted to suffering. If there was peace and happiness for them, it came only in brief snatches. And I am sure that they felt their love was proportional to how much they sacrificed for their kids.

For many years, my perception of my parents was that their identities were built on feelings of hopelessness, overshadowed by predictions that the worst was yet to come. I was always being warned of the dangers and hazards of the things I wanted to do. Then, when things didn't turn out as I had wanted, I was reminded yet again to expect and prepare for the worst. In this way, they helped to create my reality, based on the perceptions dictated by their egos, in which their most dire predictions came true.

This is not to say that there weren't light moments in our lives. On weekends we would all go fishing at a pier near our home. In the summers we went camping. One incident, which occurred at Yosemite National Park, stands out in my mind as particularly representative of my family's dictates to hurry, be fearful, and be careful, all at the same time.

Whenever we went camping, we set up two tents,

one where we slept and one where we kept the food and cooking utensils. The reason for this was to avoid attracting bears, which would usually go after whatever food they smelled. My parents had always impressed on us how dangerous bears were and how careful we had to be.

One night we were awakened by a bear that had gotten into the food tent. Since it was beside the tent where we slept, we panicked. Everybody was yelling to hurry up and get dressed, to make a run for the car, where we would be safe from the bear. I grabbed my pants, pulled them on as fast as I could, zipped them up—and, to my horror, caught my penis in the zipper!

With everyone screaming that the bear was going to attack us if we didn't hurry, my brothers and my father helped me extricate myself from the claws of my zipper. By the time we got out of the tent, the bear was gone, probably scared off by all the noise we had made. Now I look back on that experience with humor, but it serves as an excellent example for me of how always hurrying and expecting imminent danger can itself create disaster.

Because I initially bought into my parents' belief system, life became a great pressure, and I felt heavy, tired, and in danger most of the time. Happiness had no place in this philosophy. I felt guilty about the past and worried about the future. Within that framework, there was not much room to live in the present. And if I did find myself living in the present, I felt undeserving of whatever happiness I might chance to experience.

At the core of my parents' identities was Guilt with a

capital G. If I was not disappointing my father, I was hurting my mother. In growing up, I thought that my family had a monopoly on guilt.

I adopted my parents' perception that the purpose of life was to learn to suffer and survive in a fearful world where every day someone or some circumstance would threaten or attack you. In my parents' world, bad news was emphasized and good news was virtually ignored.

It is not surprising that one of the early markers on my roadmap was that I was to imitate my parents and become a workaholic. That became a powerful part of my ego. One of the first applications I had of this ethic was that I should work as hard as I could to get a good education so that I might acquire all the material things my parents were never able to have. It was not until I was an adult that I learned I was dyslexic, making formal education very difficult for me.

Part of the game plan I learned to integrate with my ego was initially to trust no one and never to give anyone the benefit of the doubt. In my family, pride, how well you performed, and what others thought of you were all prized far more than anything else.

One of the most difficult things that any of us must learn in life is which map to follow. Every day there are decisions to make in every area of our lives. And because most of us view both life and our minds as being complex, we find decision-making complex. The ego is very good at hiding from us the simple truth that all decisions are based on either love or fear. It also tries to keep us in the dark about the fact that all of our decisions lead to only one of two possible outcomes: happiness or unhappiness.

Most of my life I erroneously thought that all my decisions should be based on what I had learned by my past experiences. Based on my past, I spent more time than I like to admit deciding whom I was to fear, whom I could trust, and who was a potential enemy. I thought that all decisions were based on fear; I did not realize that a decision could be based on love.

My perception of my childhood is that my parents made 98 percent of their decisions based on fear. During most of my childhood they made all my decisions, and I was given no choices. Later, on the rare occasions when I was allowed to make decisions for myself, I had feelings of panic and was convinced that any decision I made would be wrong. Of course, I usually fulfilled these negative prophesies, proving to myself and the world that my worst fears were justified.

Our family had a weekend ritual. We would take a drive in the afternoon, and in the early evening we would go to the movies. What was interesting, was how we made the decision of which movie to see. The attraction to guilt and to suffering was so strong that when it came to making a decision, none of us could say which movie we wanted to see—because that would have caused us to feel guilty. We each tried to make the decision on the basis of what we thought the rest of the family would like to see. Usually we ended up going to

movies that no one wanted to see. We had togetherness, but it was togetherness in suffering.

Having No Maps

There doesn't seem to be much agreement in the world
about how to make decisions or what map to follow. In
one way or another most of us spend an extraordinary
amount of energy attempting to make decisions based
on satisfying the desires we perceive through our physical senses. And even when we attain those goals, the
satisfaction does not last. Over and over again we end
up feeling frustrated.

In spite of our frustrations, we continue to seek the
pleasures of the outer world, becoming attached to material objects and then finding that they do not bring us
any lasting peace or happiness.

On my journey of life, I, like so many others, developed multiple and often conflicting goals, and I tried
to juggle all of them. For example, I wanted to be a devoted husband and parent, but I also wanted to be a
physician who would give all his time to his patients.
The result was that I felt I was neglecting my patients
when I spent time with my family, and I felt neglectful
as a parent and husband when I spent time with my
patients.

My goals would shift so rapidly that I often became
confused and would forget my most immediate goal or
even lose the direction in which I thought I was going.
It was as though I had collected fragments of many
different maps and had tried to piece them together.
But they all led to destinations that had no purpose, or I

traveled for a short time along a path only to discover
that it led me nowhere at all.

I am convinced that our true state of mind is wholeness, containing only the purity of love. In that state,
our minds are joined collectively as one, and we feel
forever loved, forever loving, and forever pure. When
we isolate ourselves from love and from God, we begin
to think of ourselves as independent of God and the
world around us, separate and alone. That separated
part of the mind is the ego, filled with thoughts based
on fear and guilt, leaving very little room for love.

I have spent much of my life obeying the voice of my
ego, keeping the presence of love, the voice of love, hidden from my awareness. My attachment to guilt simply
smothered that awareness. Guilt and fear are so inter-
twined that they cannot be separated. Love and guilt
cannot exist simultaneously any more than love and
fear can.

When I listen to my ego's voice of fear and guilt, it
sounds like this: "You don't know what you're doing or
how to make decisions. Every time you make a decision, it's the wrong one. You've failed many times before and will go on failing. Besides, you should be
ashamed of yourself for the awful things you did in the
past. You are a rotten person. You deserve to suffer and
be punished. Go ahead, attack and hurt yourself again.
Admit that you're lost in life. You've made a mess of
things, and there's no way you can get out of this
mountain of garbage you created. You cannot get anywhere from here."

There is not much chance to hear the voice of love when thoughts like those come in like lightning and thunder deafening you to any other voice in your mind. And, as if that is not enough, my ego paints the picture that I am a victim of the world I see, and that the cause of all my problems is outside me. My ego does not want me to take responsibility for anything; it wants me always to blame other people.

The signposts marked out in the roadmap of my ego are worry, doubt, uncertainty, conflict, and self-righteous anger.

The map of the ego is based on "getting," and it leads us to further illusions. The map of love, on the other hand, is based on "giving," and it leads us to peace of mind.

Today there is much turmoil in the world. Many people are starving, and the specter of nuclear annihilation continues to haunt the planet. Everywhere we look there are examples that the ego can use to validate its position that the world is a terrible place, with plenty of justification for fear. Yet, as I travel around the world I find evidence of a spiritual renaissance. I hear people saying that there must be another way of looking at the world; there just has to be a better way. People are beginning to question the values that have imprisoned humankind for many centuries.

Perhaps we are discovering, at last, that the roadmap for peace is an inward one, and there is guidance within our hearts to help us on our journey, telling us how to achieve a state of mind and heart where there is only love and happiness, rather than guilt, fear, and anger.

There are really only two maps from which to choose: the map of love and the map of the ego. Every decision that each of us makes in life will be based on one of these maps.

The destination of the map of love, based on the God of love and the love of God, is eternal peace, joy, and happiness. Its singular goal is inner peace. All roads on the map lead to bridges of forgiveness, bridges that everyone must cross if they are to experience happiness. All roads on this map are filled with light.

By contrast, the map of the ego is based on the false gods of fear. All its roads lead to bridges of unforgiveness. When we cross them we find our ego's chosen destination, a place of conflict, anger, doubt, and unhappiness. All roads on this map are filled with darkness.

Remembering the Choices

It takes work to remember that we have choices. It takes discipline and a willingness to retrain our minds so that we can unlearn much of what we have learned and valued. Everything in life depends on the thoughts we choose to hold in our minds and on our willingness to change our belief systems.

We do have the freedom to choose the map of love, to believe and finally to know that our true identities are not physical but spiritual. We can begin to turn away from the limited belief systems of our egos and choose the belief that we are love, and that love is the essence of our beings. We can choose to believe that our true home is in the Heart of God, and that we have never really left our home, regardless of how it may seem.

It is up to each one of us to choose which map we will use to guide our journey. No one can choose for us. Do we choose love or do we choose fear?

I saw a weed today
that had the majesty and
beauty of the most
perfect flower.

Can it be that
Life, indeed, depends
entirely on how we choose
to perceive it?

2

THE EARLY YEARS OF MY EGO

I learned today that
when my chest feels like
it is in a vise, and
my breathing is tight,
I have inside tears
that need
to become outside tears.

The pathway of life that most of us choose is dictated by the map of the ego. The best way I know for showing how this works in our lives is to use my own life as an illustration. In doing so, I'll show you how my life changed when I began learning how to follow the map of love.

My fight with God started very early in life, and it is rekindled every time I judge and blame others or condemn myself. The battle is renewed every time I hold on to anger or a grievance with another person, or when I withhold my love from someone else or from myself. My past is filled with experiences in which these attitudes and emotions developed.

When you want something very badly and you don't get it, all the conditions are set in place to activate the ego. The ego is that part of the mind that focuses on the needs of the body and the personality. It is that part of the mind that splits us away from the spiritual self. It thrives on frustration, and its influence in our lives is kindled by the fear and guilt it creates. The ego also creates an illusion—and it truly is an illusion—of a split between ourselves and God, even though such a split is actually impossible.

I still remember the first time I consciously encountered my ego, and perhaps it was then that my fight with God actually began. I was about four years old. My brother was going out with some friends and I wanted to go with him. However, he didn't want me tagging along, and my mother supported him in this. I remember my frustration, my anger, and my tears. Although I didn't even know the meaning of the word at the time, this was my first real "grievance" with people.

I was furious at my mother and brother; in my mind, they were the cause of my upset. Although I'm sure I didn't know the word *victim* at the time, any more than I knew the word *grievance*, I'm certain that I felt victimized, and I felt my anger was completely justified. Even at that early age, I was adopting the teachings of the world around me; I was learning the ego principle that if something goes wrong in your world, you should find someone or something to blame.

I am overwhelmed as I recount the number of times I have fallen into that same pattern of behavior, both as a child and as an adult. I believed the ego's law that if you want something and don't get it, you must feel frustrated. If the frustration continues, you must feel angry, you must blame other people, and you must hold on to your anger.

As I mentioned earlier, both my parents came from families that were filled with fear and turmoil, and everyone worked extremely hard. My two brothers and I had many chores to do at home, and during holidays we worked in our parents' store. In addition, I sold magazines such as *Liberty* and *Saturday Evening Post* from door to door. There was very little time to relax. There was always more work to do, and everything was hurry, hurry, hurry.

My parents believed that the only way to accomplish anything was to do it yourself, to trust no one to do your work for you. For example, they never completely trusted the bank. They did have a bank account, but they never put all their money in it. They taught us always to be tight-lipped with people until we knew them well enough to trust them.

Although my parents considered themselves religious, we rarely went to services. God didn't seem to have much to do with how a person got through life.

Because my father had no formal education and my mother had only a limited one, they were determined that their children do well in school. I sometimes think that my parents' feelings about my education were so strong that, had they been able to, they would have gotten me into Harvard when I was in the second grade.

My brothers Les (nine years older than I) and Art (six years older) excelled in school. Years later, when I went to the same public schools they had attended, my teachers expected me to perform as my brothers had. What a disappointment I was, not only to my teachers but to my parents and myself!

My first sense of failure came in kindergarten. I flunked. All my classmates went on to the first grade while I was held back. I'm sure that some kindly explanation was given, but all I remember was feeling dumb. I was extremely shy, and I presented myself as immature, fearful, and not at all sure of myself.

One day in kindergarten I was given a note to take home. I was to be in a Christmas play and my teacher was asking my parents' permission for me to be in the chorus.

At rehearsal, the music teacher went around the room listening for someone whom she had heard singing flat. She quickly found who it was: me. She politely asked me only to "mouth" the words at the performance; under no circumstances was I to sing aloud. My ego came rushing in with all its power, and I learned what the feeling of rejection was all about. I felt as if I had a giant clamp around my stomach and the bottom of my heart. My fear and my ego voice were telling me to get used to this pain because it was going to happen over and over again.

Things got worse when I finally entered first grade. I was unable to learn to read or spell. Everything I did was wrong.

The teachers divided the students into groups according to their levels of competence. In order to disguise accomplishment levels and protect the children from the stigma of more obvious grading systems, the different groups were given names such as blue bird, black bird, and red bird. However, everyone knew what the names meant, and I had no doubt that I was in the bottom group.

I had problems taking directions of any kind. I had

no sequential memory and was not able to memorize or take more than a single direction at a time. My teachers and my parents told me that I was lazy and unmotivated.

It wasn't until I entered medical school that I discovered I had dyslexia, a specific learning disability.

My parents never had to be concerned about the grades my brothers made in school. They were both good students. But for me, school was a real struggle. I am very sure my parents were as confused about why I did so poorly as I was. The best they could do was to put more pressure on me to earn better grades. Although I am certain they didn't intend it this way, I took the pressure to mean: *We will love you a lot if you get good grades at school; we will love you less, and may even withdraw our love, if you get poor grades.*

As so often happens in education, as well as in the home, I was at least learning one thing—another law of the ego, that good performance is a prerequisite for love.

In my mind, the conditions of love were clear. Because of my performance I was not worthy of love. Clumsy and hyperactive, it seemed that regardless of how hard I tried, my performance always won me negative feedback.

With my ego fully engaged, I soon became familiar with the adult world's way of measuring and evaluating me. Since that world attacked me for poor performance, I quickly learned to condemn and attack myself.

I remember learning about lies when I was a child. It was all very confusing to me. I particularly remember one day when my mother was lecturing me about honesty. At that point, someone knocked at the door. My mother asked me to answer it and to tell whoever was there that she was not at home. I naively said, "But that is a lie!" She replied, "It is not a lie at all. It is a *white lie* and white lies are okay because they don't hurt anyone."

I began to learn that my parents were human and they did not always practice what they preached. And I began to learn how little they trusted themselves. All during this time, my ego was teaching me to distrust myself, other people, and God.

Learning the Laws of the World

When I was five years old, I discovered that nothing lasted forever. The concept of dying had not entered my mind and I think I believed there was really no such thing as death.

We had a neighbor, a man who had been ill for some time. When one day I realized that I had not seen him for a while, I asked my parents where he was. They said that he had died. They explained that he had gone to *heaven*, but this did not satisfy me. Nevertheless, I was left with the thought that someday I would die and that would be the end of me. I would no longer be with my parents and my family. It was too awful to think about, so I buried it in the back of my mind until many years later.

I was always confused about male and female roles as a child, and that confusion continued into my adult life. As I look back, I see that I have always been fearful of intimate relationships with members of the opposite sex. During those few times that I have chosen to have close relationships with women, I usually picked women who were similar to my mother. As far as male friends were concerned, I always had a large number of superficial friends, but would rarely let anyone get close to my heart.

As an adolescent I wore so many disguises to prevent the world from knowing who I really was that I didn't know who I was myself. My life was filled with contradictions and hypocrisy.

One of the greatest contradictions was that I was as shy as a person could be, and yet I was a leader of my high school pep squad. This was just one of the ways that I tried to cover up the fact that inside this shell called the body was a very dumb and inadequate person. I was also a very conforming person—or tried to be—and I spent more time than I like to remember trying to be an obedient son. It was difficult for me to take risks or make decisions, and in fact my parents made most decisions for me.

At sixteen, when my friend died in an automobile accident, I made my first major decision on my own. With very little faith in God anyway, that senseless death seemed to offer proof that I could not believe in God any more. I decided that I would never again go to religious services. For the first time in my life, my parents were unable to change my mind.

My decision did not leave me with a contented or peaceful mind. On the contrary, I was filled with anger, resentment, and conflict.

In spite of many confusing ego messages, I can now look back on my high school days and see that even then I was not without inner guidance. I remember writing an essay about what I wanted to do in life. My grammar and sentence structure were poor, but my teacher congratulated me on the sincerity of the content. In the essay I told how I wanted to be a physician, to make a difference by helping others.

Even then I was receiving guidance to become a psychiatrist. I suspect that in becoming a psychiatrist I wanted to help myself by getting to know and help the fearful child within me. As I look back on it, I think that part of what influenced me in this came from my mother. When I was growing up, there was a radio program called *Ask Mr. Anthony*. It was one of the early talk shows where people called in to get help with problems in their lives. It was my mother's favorite program and she listened to it often. Perhaps, in its own way, that program was a roadmap for both our lives.

To the ego, life is a game of hide-and-seek.
We hide the love that is within us from ourselves
and then we seek it outside ourselves, where
it can never be found.

CHAPTER

3

THE
BATTLE
CONTINUES

Just as silence is the footprint of God,
so chatter, noise, and the business of
the world are the footprints
of the ego.

During my early adult years, my fight with God reached its peak. My ego convinced me that the world was a most painful place, and I became increasingly preoccupied with my fear of rejection. My way of life, as I followed my fragmented and often conflicted road-map, continued to illustrate the truth that *you get what you expect*. I fully believed that if something bad was going to happen to someone, I would be that someone.

Although part of me rejected God, another part of my mind felt that God was punishing me for all my misdeeds. I also believed that I was being punished for things I didn't even know I had done.

There is no room for peace of mind or love in our hearts when the ego is telling us to value anger and hate. The moment we accept the belief that we are victims, fear and anger dominate our lives. In my early adult years, I would repeatedly find situations that confirmed, at least in my eyes, that I was a victim and that my anger was not only rational but healthy. When anger seems justified, we can be sure of one thing at least: peace of mind is not our goal. I have spent an enormous amount of time during my life seeking justification for my anger. If you look hard enough, you can find it every time another person doesn't give you what you want and every time things don't go exactly your way. Although I thought that I wanted peace of mind, time and time again my actions proved that this was not my goal.

Are We Here to Help or to Kill?

World War II broke out just one year before I was graduated from high school. I was seventeen years old—eligible for the draft. I was petrified that I might have to kill another person or be killed. The whole notion of war was insane to me, so insane that I seriously considered becoming a conscientious objector, even though I realized that such a decision would have been considered unpatriotic and would have earned me the wrath and rejection of almost everyone I knew.

About this time some of my friends and I heard about the navy's new V-12 program designed to send students to college and medical school, whereupon they would end up as officers. It seemed to offer a solution to my problems, since it would allow me to go on with my education, would allow me to be helpful and would exempt me from combat.

After some difficulties, I was accepted into the program and was sent to the University of California in Berkeley, California for pre-medical training, and was later sent to Stanford Medical School. I was filled with tremendous fear about being able to make it in college, and part of me was convinced that I would fail. It was there that I eventually discovered that my reading problems were due to dyslexia. Somehow, in a way that I still don't understand, I was able to muck through. Perhaps it was sheer determination, a trait I had learned from my parents for which I am very grateful.

❦

In 1944 I was assigned to a naval hospital near Oakland, and there I learned another lesson about the ways that our thoughts create our realities. I was working on the ward for mental patients. My chief duty was giving enemas and cleaning the toilets for Saturday's captain's inspection. The captain had a white glove, which he ran over every surface. If he found any dust or dirt on it, your weekend pass was canceled. Needless to say, I spent most weekends at the hospital.

Months later, I was transferred to the laboratory. After a short training period, I was assigned the task of examining the feces of every patient who entered the hospital. Four weeks later, the head of the department was transferred and I was assigned his position. My friends instantly gave me the title "Head Shit Man."

If you believe in your ego, as I did in those days, then you believe that the past will accurately predict the future. So I saw this event as prophetic: surely it meant that I was destined to live in the bowels of the world. My ego was once again telling me that if there was a God, he could only be an unloving, punishing one.

❦

After entering medical school, I found that I was required to do a tremendous amount of memorization, which was very difficult for me because of my dyslexia. I had to work harder than others just to keep up. My ego had a field day because we took examinations so often. The competition was extreme, and my feelings of inadequacy kept me in a constant state of fear. When you are attached to such feelings and they seem very real, the thoughts of the ego will not allow you to believe that it is possible to find peace of mind.

Histology was particularly difficult for me because of my spatial confusion as a dyslexic. However, I did well in anatomy, where I could use my kinesthetic memory and so didn't have to rely on memorization. I did quite well in clinical medicine and caring for patients, too, because I was very intuitive.

Still, every minute of medical school was a struggle for me. I was graduated in 1950, near the bottom of my class, with my low self-esteem intact.

I still bought into the map of my ego, which told me that my purpose in life was to suffer. During most of my life I found little evidence to refute that belief. There was only one exception that I can recall, which a question asked by my dear friend Hugh Prather prompted me to remember.

"Jerry," he said, "I know that you were a militant atheist during most of your life. But was there ever a time that just for an instant you felt the presence of God, the presence of Light?"

What flashed into my mind was an incident that happened in 1948, during my fourth year in medical school. It was 3:00 A.M. and I was assisting in the delivery of a baby. It was my first delivery and I had no idea how it would affect me. As the baby emerged, it was as if an unimaginably brilliant light illuminated the delivery room. This light had nothing to do with the electrical lights in the room.

To this day I can easily recall the joy, the awe, and the excitement of that moment. I felt that the whole universe was joined in happiness and love, witnessing the birth of that child. The experience was beyond the grasp of my intellect. There was an awakening of a fire of love and happiness in my heart that I had never known until that moment.

I knew with certainty that for that precious timeless moment we—the mother, the child, the nurse, and I— were experiencing the presence of God.

Unfortunately, the words *God* and *love* are not often heard in most medical schools.

That exquisite feeling I experienced with the birth lasted until 8:00 A.M., when it quickly disappeared as I returned to the usual business of the world and the rat race of medical school where I found myself, once again, analyzing everything.

❧

I interned at the U.S. Public Health Hospital in Brighton, Massachusetts. It was an excellent rotating internship and we had the best consultants from the top universities. There were no tests, no competition; to me, that meant that for the first time in years I was in a friendly environment.

I found myself totally immersed in my work, putting in long hours and enjoying it. It's amazing to me that when you are engrossed in helping others, your self-concerns seem to evaporate. Except for the month that I was on the tuberculosis ward, I was relatively free of my old sidekicks, fear and panic. And after surviving mouth-to-mouth resuscitation on a woman who had tuberculosis, my old fear of dying from that disease disappeared.

I had no social life, but I didn't really mind. In fact, it was a happy time for me. I spent such long hours on the ward that there was very little time for my ego to take off on its preoccupations with all my negative traits. I had a bedside manner that seemed to bring comfort to my patients. They knew that I cared, and they did well under my care. I began to feel that maybe I had something to offer this world.

It has been said many times by spiritual leaders that the best way to experience peace of mind is to become immersed in helping others. When you spend just one moment putting the interests of another soul above your own, that is the moment when God's presence can be felt most strongly. I now believe that on an unconscious level I was feeling just that, but my old resistance to God was so strong that I didn't let myself know that.

My view of myself was that I still had inside me that clumsy child of my past. In carving a turkey or cutting a steak, the chances were high that everything would end up on the floor. Imagine my surprise, then, when the chief surgeon took a special interest in me. He treated me more like a son than an intern, giving me confidence that there was nothing that I couldn't do. Although all the other interns merely assisted, he had me doing operations while he assisted.

I performed all kinds of surgeries—tonsillectomies,

appendectomies, hernia repairs. My fingers were nimble. I was extremely dextrous, and there were no signs of the old "clumsy Jerry." Here was yet another miracle in my life, though I still didn't allow that word in my vocabulary. I found myself doing things that I had never thought I could.

The chief of surgery thought I would make a great surgeon and was disappointed when I told him I still wanted to become a psychiatrist.

I now see that experience as one of the most powerful events in my life. It was the first time I had the opportunity to work with a fatherlike figure who had complete confidence in my abilities. Of course, there was still that negative voice inside me with its one-word vocabulary—*can't*. But for the first time I experienced unconditional love and acceptance. The chief of surgery provided me with a stepping-stone, preparing me for what was to happen to me many years later when I began consciously to accept God's unconditional love.

The Ego's Law of the "Double Lose"

At the end of my internship we discovered that the staff had secretly been grading us on our performance. To my astonishment, I had been selected as the number-one intern. I'm certain that if I had known I was being graded, my fear and anxiety would have severely hampered my performance.

One might think that my success would have given me great joy, but my ego would have none of that. On hearing the news, the voice of my ego shouted at me: "If they knew what you were really like underneath that disguise you wear, if they knew how rotten and inadequate you really are, you would never get this award. For all that you have done in your life, you deserve to suffer and be punished, not rewarded."

So I learned that my ego had still another rule: that I should be afraid not only of failure but of success. As far as my ego was concerned, I should suffer for both success and failure. No matter what I did, my ego was determined to make it a "lose-lose" situation.

I took on tons of stress, just to feel alive. The word *relax* was hardly in my vocabulary. Even then, it was clear that I was becoming a workaholic, like my parents. I never walked; I ran. It almost felt like a sin when I tried to relax. In complete obedience to my ego, I shunned happiness. I continued to think that my behavior was genetic and there was nothing I could do to change. My ego had me in its vise.

My struggle with God was often a subtle one. The voice of fear was the only voice I thought there was. At least it was the only voice I chose to pay attention to. While I continued to make fear my idol, the thought of God still remained far from my mind.

I have been told that patience is a virtue.
If that is true, it means that I have been
without virtue most of my life.

LAWS
OF SCARCITY

Possessiveness is the soul of the ego,
which is limitless in its desire
to own both people and things.

In 1953, I was married to Pat Powell. Twenty years later we divorced. The years following that divorce were not easy for either of us. We both found it difficult to let go of past hurts, and we both worked hard to bring harmony and love back into our relationship.

I am delighted to say that today the old tensions have disappeared between us. We respect and love each other dearly. Faultfinding and blame have vanished.

Not long ago, over lunch, Pat showed me pictures that she recently took of our first grandchild, Jacquelyn Armour Jampolsky.

I shared with her a rough draft of my new book, asking for her comments and for her approval of my including sections about our life together. As we discussed these things, I thought what wonderful teachers we have been for each other, for learning forgiveness and acceptance. We both trust that as dear lifetime friends we will always be there for each other, both in good times and in bad. It is clear that we truly want the best for each other.

I am so grateful for this healing between us. There was a time when I could never have imagined that it could occur.

My struggle over my marriage and divorce taught me that a fundamental law of the ego is the law of scarcity. In relationships, this law implies that somehow you were put on earth with something missing, and you are supposed to find a person who can supply that missing piece. You form that relationship so that you can feel complete.

Following my internship in Boston, I returned to San Francisco, where I was assistant and then chief resident in neuropsychiatry at Stanford-Lane Hospital.

Although I was quickly gaining confidence as a physician, I continued to be shy in social situations and had difficulty even asking for a date. My fear of rejection always stopped me. It was then that I met Pat.

It took a lot of courage to ask her to go out with me, and I was more than surprised when she accepted. Pat was everything I had ever dreamed of in a woman. In my eyes she was the most beautiful woman I had ever met. She was extremely intelligent, and, most important, she really cared about people.

Pat was a speech therapist at Children's Hospital in Oakland; she also had a private practice. She was one of the friendliest people I'd ever met. I found her very easy to be with, and we had much in common. We went on many picnics and on long walks on the beach. We enjoyed nature, we enjoyed being alone together, and we loved to dance.

We fell madly in love. I had never allowed myself to be so close to anyone, and it was the first time I truly felt in love. The courtship also had its stormy times. Now and then, when the closeness and growing intimacy of our relationship began to frighten me, I would create arguments, or I would run away.

I was amazed that she actually enjoyed my company. My ego was gratified because I still looked upon myself as a clumsy, ugly duckling, and here was an attractive, intelligent woman who actually cared for me. My ego, which had caused me to feel so empty inside, saw in Pat all the things that I thought were missing in me: beauty, intelligence, social grace, and the ability to love.

At the parties we attended during our courtship I was quite dependent on Pat to carry on most social interactions. She was so good at that. In a sense I think the little boy in me was hiding behind Pat's apron strings. It was as if she created for me a disguise in which I could appear normal and socially presentable.

We had a wonderful wedding and honeymoon. During the first part of our life together, I was stationed at Travis Air Force Base, during the Korean conflict, and I commuted to our home in San Francisco, a lovely but inexpensive apartment on Russian Hill.

We both worked very hard at our jobs. Pat was an

excellent cook and we entertained often. While Pat formed many close friendships, I kept mine at a very superficial level. I still couldn't allow myself to have the closeness of friendships in which I felt safe opening my heart.

During those years, if someone had dared suggest to me that I was self-centered, I would have vehemently denied it. I saw myself as a hardworking physician who helped many people. How blind we can be! Now, when I look back, I see that the marriage focused on my needs and my schedule. And although I have had trouble admitting it to myself in the past, my work came first and my marriage and family came second. Pat and I had many arguments about this, but I simply rationalized that most successful doctors ran their lives just as I did.

I now see how extremely chauvinistic I was. And yet, there was that other part of me that saw myself as weak and always giving in to Pat on major decisions.

A marriage based on selfish interests or in which the male is dominant is a relationship with much fear in it. And that fear stems from the fear of love. All of the above was true for me, but my ego and its intense near-sightedness kept me asleep and protected me from the truth.

The early years of our marriage started with double martinis; later I turned to scotch on the rocks. Although I didn't see it at the time, I was becoming an alcoholic. I convinced myself that I was just a social drinker, perhaps a heavy drinker, but certainly not an alcoholic. Once again I made excuses, to myself and others, for my behavior. The voice of my ego told me that all my friends drank the same amount I did, and none of them were alcoholics. Because I never drank in the daytime, I felt sure that I was in control of my drinking. But I wasn't.

❦

Our son Greg was born on July 26, 1955. My memory is that Pat and I could not have been happier with that event and with the birth of our second son, Lee, two years later. The kids were great. Pat was a wonderful mother, and I was delighted with being a father—though admittedly I wasn't home very much. In fact, Pat began complaining because I was so seldom home, but I brushed her complaints aside; I felt that a physician's responsibility was to meet the needs of his patients first and his family second.

In the summers, we took camping trips, rented houseboats, and went fishing with the kids. Carmel, California, was our favorite place to relax. Eventually we bought property there and spent many happy times on the beach and playing tennis.

Sometimes tragedy, in an unexpected way, can bring people closer together. When our children were very young, our home in Tiburon burned. The children were in the house at the time. Pat was at the dentist's office and I was at work. I rushed home to find the kids safe, but more than half of the house was destroyed.

The only thing that mattered to Pat and me was that our boys were safe. But sifting through the ashes was devastating for both of us. Nearly all the material things we valued were gone.

In the midst of the tragedy, I did not want to be dependent on anyone. When people offered help, I told them that everything was under control, which was far from the truth. I now thank God that a few people refused to listen to me and gave us shelter and clothes.

Before the fire, our marital problems had been getting worse, but then a new bond began growing between us. We lived in temporary quarters for about six months, during which we began to reexamine our values. We found that we previously had put the wrong things, such as money, at the top of our list. Things that had been at the bottom of our list now began to appear at the top. Unfortunately, however, about a year after the fire, we fell back into our old patterns.

I kept long hours at the office and hospital, hours that went far beyond counting. I began to think of Pat as a complainer, but now I see that I was the complainer but I denied my feelings and projected them onto Pat. How tricky and deceptive the ego can be! When you think you have got ahold of it, it slips out of your hands, just like a slippery fish.

In spite of the long hours at work, I stayed involved in my sons' activities, attending Little League games, parents' night at school, and the like. I tried to live up to the image of a devoted and loving father. I convinced myself that I was close to my children and that I shared my love openly with them.

In retrospect, I see that I didn't share the center of my being with the boys, with Pat, or with anyone else. The nights that I did spend at home were usually spent under the influence of alcohol, so I really wasn't available to my family in the way that I wanted to believe I was.

I had a Dr. Jekyll and Mr. Hyde personality. In the haven of my office I could be loving and receive love. But at home I was quite capable of being a tyrant, denying it even as I was doing it. At the office I could talk about unconditional love with parents; at home, I was always nagging my sons to get good grades in school. In spite of my good intentions, I was doing exactly those things that I had so sharply criticized in my parents.

The maps of our egos and the laws of the world would have us believe that success is measured by our bank accounts, our possessions, and what others think about us. The voice of the ego says that our success depends on how clever we have been at manipulating people and stepping over them on our climb to the top.

I did all the things my parents had taught me to do. Without realizing it, I was still afraid not to follow their roadmaps. I worked hard. I made a lot of money. I had many prized possessions. I was respected by my colleagues. And above all, I had a beautiful wife and wonderful children.

The Role of Fear in Marriage

In truth, I chose to listen to my ego's voice of fear most of the time. When I felt joy, it was fleeting at best; guilt would rush in to destroy it. My ego was still telling me that I did not have the right to be happy.

The ego will tell us to run, run, run, but it will never tell us what we are running toward. It will tell us that the only success worth having is to be found in the outer world. So, as I followed my ego's map, I was always running, and even under the guise of helping others I was thinking of myself first.

I collected all those trophies of the material world, all the things that were supposed to make me happy. Meanwhile, I hid my injured heart from everyone, including myself. How could others possibly get close to me when I would not allow myself to be aware of and close to myself!

In the early 1970s, I became severely depressed and disillusioned with my life. The things that were supposed to bring me happiness weren't working. Although I didn't realize it at the time, I was suffering from spiritual emptiness. So another law of the ego began to rule my behavior: "If something is going wrong in your life, find someone to blame."

I began to blame Pat for my unhappiness, and I found a hundred and one things to make her wrong. Of course, she had done nothing wrong. The "wrong" was my own perception, and I projected all my self-hate, resentment, and disappointment onto her. I made things so unbearable that our marriage lost all the life it once had. Pat tried everything to keep our marriage together, but I had given up hope.

To my utter surprise, other people looked upon us as the model of a successful, happy, loving family.

Pat would say many times that she gave 80 percent in the marriage, and I gave only 20. I didn't agree with her then, but I certainly do now. Pat was willing to put all of herself into the marriage. Because I was seldom around, she went back to school to study interior design and launched a new career. And the more successful she became, the more threatened I became. In 1973, our twenty-year marriage ended in divorce.

It was one of the most painful experiences of my life. Although we were no longer living together, Pat and I continued to argue about money, possessions, and who was right. Still denying my alcoholism, repression and suppression became the main game of my ego. My emotional pain was so great that I would do anything to hide it from my awareness. I had almost no insight into how disturbed I really was. Harboring unforgiving thoughts, Pat and I continued to blame each other for many years to come.

I knew I was upset, but I did not realize what a roaring volcano I had inside me or how self-destructive I was. My drinking grew steadily worse. My back problems, too, intensified, causing me great physical pain. I pretended it had no psychological significance because my X rays showed that I had an organic back disease. How blind and deaf we can be!

My ego danced, telling me I was unlovable and could not trust others. And through my behavior I continued to find that the world was as unsafe and unloving as I perceived it. I convinced myself that everyone, at a moment's notice, was ready to attack or reject me.

Perhaps subconsciously, as a way of proving that my ego was correct, I would sometimes let people get a little close to me and would listen to them as they shared their concern about my drinking. I would even "go on the wagon" and stop drinking for a few days to satisfy them. Then I would start drinking even more heavily. My friends became angry, gave up on me, and many disappeared from my life.

Whenever a friend disappeared from my life, my ego would say to me, "See, you can't trust anyone. There is no such thing as unconditional love. How can anyone care about you when you're so unlovable! You deserve to feel guilty for being such a bad person." And then my ego would say, "By the way, a scotch on the rocks would quickly get rid of the guilt you're feeling." So once again I would listen to the wrong voice and go back to booze. I rationalized that if I could not control people so that they would love me, I could at least control them by provoking them into rejecting me.

What a hypocrisy my life became! I was an alcoholic, yet I had a reputation in my community as an excellent therapist, especially for alcoholics.

Another law that the ego would have us follow is that we are each separate entities, each with a separate mind in a world without intimacy, a world filled with a sense of separation and aloneness. Because I wore a disguise of friendliness, complete with a plastic smile, I doubt that anyone knew how lonely I really was. I was lonely when I was with my children, when I was with my wife, even when I was in a crowd.

I had a feeling of separateness and alienation not only from other people and from the world but even from my body. I felt uncomfortable in my body because I continued to see myself as clumsy and awkward. I held on to childhood feelings of not belonging anywhere. All my life I had a longing, hopeless feeling of being home-less, a feeling of always looking for a niche, a place of safety. Even as I sought this place, I was convinced I would never find it.

As I look back, I think that I spent most of my life in a state of chronic agitation, unhappiness, depression, and hopelessness. Even as an adult, while most of the world saw me as highly successful, I still had the same perception of my life. My outer success did not change the inner state of my mind and heart. Part of me kept insisting that there had to be more to life than this.

I do not remember consciously thinking that I was a seeker or that I was looking for my home and for peace of mind. But I do remember well that chronic state of emptiness and sadness, superimposed on giant pools of dammed-up *inside tears*. In nearly every area of my life, I felt that no one really understood me. And I understood nothing at all!

Spiritual Deprivation

If someone had told me at the time of my divorce that my real problem was not in my relationship with my wife but in my relationship with God, I would not for a moment have believed them. It was not until many years later, when I met with Mother Teresa, that I was able to look at this differently.

Mother Teresa said that the biggest problem facing the world today is not people dying in the streets of Calcutta, and not inflation, but what she calls "spiritual deprivation." She described this as a feeling of emptiness associated with feeling separate from God and from all our brothers and sisters on planet Earth.

I can now look back at my marriage and divorce and know that underneath my depression, my self-anger, and my alcoholism was this state of spiritual deprivation that Mother Teresa described. I believe that the emptiness many of us feel is due to our battle with God, which results in our feeling separated from the Source.

> Jealousy is an accomplice of the ego
> that turns the illusion of love
> into hate.

CHAPTER
5

LIFE
IN THE
QUICKSAND

When I am depressed, somewhere deep inside,
I know that I am denying the Presence of God.

It is not easy for me to recapture what I was thinking and feeling following my separation and divorce, but looking back on it helps me to understand the influence of my ego's roadmap on my life. I kept things locked in separate vaults within my mind, so that I was unaware of what I was really thinking and feeling. To say I was numb would be an understatement.

What I do remember is that I would not have thought it possible to feel more guilty—and yet more guilt continued to pour down on me. Following the law of my ego that said I deserved to be punished, my ego continued its dance, and my back pain became almost incapacitating. No matter what I did, I felt miserable. I drank more and more. I no longer saw old friends.

During my separation and divorce, at first I actually looked forward to being by myself. But I quickly tired of TV dinners and long evenings alone. Solitude threatened me, and I ended up hating it. I kept the radio or television blasting almost all the time, even when I was not paying attention to them. The noise allowed me to escape from my conflicted thoughts and created the illusion that I wasn't alone.

If anyone had asked me what life was all about, I probably would have answered from the center of my ego, "Life is surviving and suffering, and if you have brief moments of happiness you're just one of the lucky ones."

I was desperate for companionship. I hated playing the dating game, but I did it anyhow. I purposely kept my relationships very superficial. I learned another of the ego's laws—that by focusing on the body you can keep your mind away from God.

At middle age, all of my old adolescent drives and fears resurfaced. My focus on sex had very little to do with love. There was that old enemy, my ego, disguised as a friend, telling me, "Go out and prove to yourself that you are desirable and lovable."

The empty quality of my relationships, devoid of commitment or true caring, served only to make me feel more guilty and depressed. My self-esteem was in the pits. To drown my depression, my alcohol consumption increased even more.

I was exhausted and suicidal, but I was afraid of dying. In spite of my internal chaos, I was, to my amazement, able to continue my practice and be helpful to others.

It seemed that I was fixated in childhood. I was reliving my childhood fears over and over again. Sometimes the experiences I was having looked brand new to me— but time showed that they were just boring reruns of the same old movies. Maybe the form had changed, but the content hadn't. It seemed as if I was determined not to learn from my experiences.

One thing I did learn from that period of my life was that the ego's capacity for self-punishment has no bounds. Even when you're really down, crawling on your belly and feeling you can't crawl another inch, the ego will come marching in to heap more punishment on you. It amazes me how weary I was able to make myself.

Every time I followed the map of the ego, I found value in guilt and further self-punishment, and if I wasn't hurting myself I would manage to hurt other people. I never once recognized how afraid of love and of God I was. I had learned the lessons of my childhood well.

Like so many people, I have a hidden (but sometimes not so hidden) fearful child that I carry around inside me. As an adult, I sometimes felt sorry for myself and pouted when I didn't get my way, just as I had when I was a child. Unable to recognize my childish behavior, I was great at detecting it in others.

Projection—denying what is inside ourselves only to see it in others—is the core of the ego. It is a mechanism that says, "The enemy is outside ourselves."

I finally stopped all social interaction for several months. A little later I took a course in photography and threw all my energy into becoming an amateur photographer, even developing and printing my own photographs.

After that I became interested in parapsychology and nontraditional healing. I began to do research in these fields, studying psychic phenomena in children, investigating Kirlian photography, and being a part of a medical team that was studying famous healers. At the same time, I began to do research in biofeedback technology, and later presented one of the first papers on the use of biofeedback in the public school system. There was something inside me that was saying there must be another way of healing.

I then went on a first-class ego trip looking for prestige and acceptance. I was invited to give lectures in Sweden and in the Soviet Union. Although my lectures were well received, I still had within me that awful feeling: "If they only knew how much I don't know!"

❦

Eventually I found myself in a relationship that any schoolboy would have known was doomed to failure. At a medical convention, I met a woman with whom I fell madly and hopelessly in love. Neither of us went to many of the professional functions, choosing instead to spend our time together.

In a strange and inexplicable way, this woman saw something in me that I didn't recognize in myself. She was able to look past my drinking and my ego to see my potential for making a difference in this world.

I was able to share things with her that I had never shared with anyone else. This was a real turning point for me. I felt the birth of a little kernel of hope, and I began to believe, along with her, that I had something to offer to the world, and that perhaps, just *perhaps*, I was lovable. I will forever be grateful to her for that spark of light that she ignited in me.

However, there was one big problem: she was married. I perceived my behavior as despicable, immoral, and unforgivable. It was completely at odds with my code of ethics. I knew what I was supposed to do, but I seemed unable to help myself. It was like falling into quicksand. There was a part of me that was saying, "You're sinking and going to die and whoever is with you is going to suffer the same consequences."

Part of me felt absolute terror. And there was my ego voice again, this time delivering what I deceived myself into believing was a brand-new message: "It's about time you had some joy and pleasure in your life. Go ahead and enjoy your new relationship. But know that you can't really enjoy it, because it will never last."

Consciously, I knew my behavior was insane. And yet, I felt as though there was a magnet pulling me more and more deeply into the relationship. Once again, my ego map had taken me right into another double-lose situation.

You can never have peace in a relationship built on deception, especially when you already know that deception is a cornerstone of the ego. But I ignored that, hoping that everything would somehow work out. I did not want to acknowledge that it is the wish to deceive that makes for discord and war. As time went on, it turned out to be a love/hate relationship. We created the illusion of love when we met each other's needs; and we created hatred and conflict when we failed to meet each other's needs.

It was a roller-coaster relationship, alternating between heights of pleasure and depths of hell. My mind continued to be compartmentalized, with no connection between its parts. Most of the time I was able to hide from my awareness the fact that I was being deceptive. But even beyond the problems of deception were the old problems of the ego, such as jealousy, possessiveness, manipulation, and the desire to control. And although I thought I wanted to give, I was still more interested in what I was getting—or not getting.

I wondered if there was a sick part of me that needed conflict in order to reassure me that I was alive. As unhealthy as I knew our relationship was, I continued to feel immobilized when it came to breaking it off. The breakup came when another man entered the picture and I was replaced. The salt of rejection poured into old wounds newly exposed. Pain and misery became my partners once again. I had only one thought about God—that his wrath was making its mark on me once again.

My bitterness over being rejected hung on for months. Today I can attest to the miracle that comes from forgiving others and yourself. Rather than continuing to feel that I had committed an unpardonable sin in that relationship, I now perceive that I made a mistake, an error to be corrected. Today that relationship is healed, and we are trusted friends.

The ego can be like glue that attaches itself to everything it touches. It can have us make relationships into idols that keep us separate from God. In my own mind, I had made an idol of that relationship, allowing my peace of mind to be dependent on what the other person did or did not do for me.

I resisted over and over again the lesson that every

time I hand over to another person the power to determine my happiness, I will end up in agony and conflict. I was not ready to learn the lesson that every time I let my ego be attached to someone or something, or make an idol of someone, I put greater distance between God and me.

After licking my wounds, I decided that I was not put in this world to have an intimate relationship. I vowed that I would be celibate. This did not make me any happier. I made that decision only because I thought that it would protect me from further pain. My depression and drinking continued. I continued to work in my office, seeing patients and doing research. In my office my disguise was patched together with Band-Aids, giving the illusion that I was "together." Feelings of hopelessness, futility, and a deep belief that I was beyond any kind of help deepened.

I felt that only a miracle could help me, yet a miracle was about the last thing in the world I could believe in. I was not at all prepared for the events that were to take place in May 1975.

I know that projection is a mirror, not a fact,
but when I am fearful, everything I see in the world
looks very real, indeed, to me.

6

CLIMBING
THE MOUNTAIN

How deceived was I
to think that what I feared
was in the world
instead of my mind.
—*A Course in Miracles*

When you are trying to put in a call to God, it doesn't matter which telephone you use. Just as there are many paths that lead to the top of the mountain, so there are many paths that lead to God.

In May 1975 I felt completely lost and had just about given up all hope. I was not consciously putting in a call to God, but nevertheless it happened. It was on this date that I was introduced to *A Course in Miracles*, an event that truly was a miracle for me, and one that helped me find my path to God.

Although part of me continued to resist, an inner part knew I was being given a valuable roadmap and a direction to travel. In some way I recognized that the vibrations of the writings in the *Course* and the vibrations of my heart were the same. I realized that these writings were not necessarily attractive or useful for everyone, but I clearly saw the *Course* as a tool for my spiritual transformation. Somehow, deep inside me, I felt that my discovery of the *Course* was a very important experience, and somehow I knew that I had found what I'd been seeking all my life.

A Tool for Spiritual Transformation

What attracted me about the *Course* was that it offered a self-study program for one's own spiritual awakening. The purpose of the *Course* was to remove blocks to the awareness of love's presence. I learned that its emphasis was love and forgiveness and I recognized how lacking I was in both.

In one of my earliest readings in the *Course*, one phrase leaped out at me: "simplicity is very difficult for a twisted mind to understand." All of this spoke to me in ways that nothing I had read before had ever done. The *Course* offered me a very specific roadmap telling how to go home to God. Its most powerful message to me was that we have separated ourselves from God and love, and that we need to awaken from our dream state of living in an illusory, perceptual world filled with fear, loneliness, and separateness, where we suffer from lack of love.

The *Course* suggests that it is possible for each of us to learn to live one second at a time, as if each second is an eternal moment. In this eternal moment we can learn to surrender to love by listening to the voice of God telling us what to think, say, and do. In this way, the peace of God becomes our only goal, and forgiveness becomes our only function. Its writings show us the way to see only the light of love in everyone, and we exclude no one from our love.

Although my initial response to the *Course* was a positive one, I found it difficult to grasp the full significance of the concept of living one second at a time. As always, whenever anything beautiful happened to me, I immediately felt a tug of war with my ego.

My ego chattered away at me, something like this: "Are you crazy? These books [the *Course*] are about God, and you know there's no such thing as God. Pay no attention to all this. *A Course of Miracles!* What a dumb title! And look at how thick these books are. You're such a slow reader, you'll never have the patience to get through them."

Sometimes, while studying the readings from the *Course*, my ego would preach at me with its own sermons: "There is no way to find peace in this world. You've tried everything, and nothing has worked for you. Accept the fact that you came into this world doomed to suffer. There is no way out of your pain. Just give up now."

Thank God I did not listen to that voice! In spite of all my resistance, I knew I had found a roadmap that was going to change my life.

There were many times when I wanted to throw the books into the ocean, even while a part of me recognized that the truth had been spoken. I thought that I must have a very confused and twisted mind indeed, because I found the spiritual path neither simple nor easy. My ego seems to put up a great fuss whenever I attempt to change a belief system. But I am not unique in this. Virtually everyone who has chosen a spiritual path in life has found the required *unlearning* both difficult and painful. I am certain it is this unlearning, more than the learning, that gives the most trouble.

Despite my resistance, I began to see that my life became much simpler when I viewed it from the perspective of the *Course*. One of the most important insights for me was that there are really only two alternatives to consider: the thought system of the ego, and the thought system of love. The ego's thought system is fueled by guilt, fear, and unforgiveness, and has a belief either that there is no God or that there is a vengeful, unloving God. Our egos thrive on making us believe that our bodies are our only realities, and that death is real and the end of all life.

Ambiguity, ambivalence, depression, doubt, pain, misery, and suffering are at the center of the ego and its insatiable desire to *get*. Conflict and war are its goals. It teaches fear, blame, attack, and defense. The ego would have us constantly see value in guilt while it tries to convince us that we will never be free of conflict. It would have us seek someone to blame or condemn whenever something goes wrong.

When we adhere to the belief system of love, and have thoughts only of God, we begin to understand why our true identities are ultimately found in our love rather than in our bodies. We are each the essence of love. Peace and happiness are at the center of the heart of love. There is a complete absence of fear and guilt, and there is no pain or misery; there are only loving and forgiving thoughts. Within this belief system, love and life are eternal, and there is no death.

❦

Perhaps one of the most valuable lessons I have learned on my spiritual path has been what the *Course* calls "special relationships." What I learned here helped me to see why my relationships had been so difficult and what I could do to change.

I began to understand that "special relationships" are those that are based on the ego's law of scarcity, which says that love is an exchange struck up between people, based on the belief that the other person can provide something that we are missing in ourselves. In order to feel whole, we seek a person who will complete us. Special relationships deny God because they would have us believe that we should love one person more than any other in the world. It is a denial of God, because God loves every one of us maximally, to the same degree.

In looking back at many of my relationships, I saw that the unconscious guilt I felt when I separated myself from God was camouflaged by the special relationship. I denied my guilt and projected it onto the other person. During the honeymoon period of feeling excited and "made whole" by the other's presence in my life, everything was fine. But that period seldom lasted long. What looked like love in the beginning frequently turned into love/hate when I began to feel that my self-centered needs were no longer being met.

Through the *Course* I began to see another possibility for a relationship. The *Course* calls it the "holy relationship," defined as "a relationship based on giving and joining, rather than getting and separation." It is when two people come together as whole individuals, experiencing no lack, and where the purpose of the relationship is to experience God. It is a relationship in which the thought of God comes first and where we include all others in our love rather than reserving our love for a single person. Put more simply, holy relationships are ones that are inclusive, not exclusive. They are relationships that are built on unconditional love for everyone, not on conditional love for one other person. It is a relationship based on acknowledging God by offering both wills as one to God and being of service in helping and loving each other.

"Perception Is a Mirror, Not a Fact"

One of the most liberating spiritual insights that came to me through the *Course* is that our perceptions are mirrors of our inner minds; they are not *facts*. Our egos keep us separate from God by projecting our perceptions onto other people. We do this by denying that we are the creators of our perceptions and by acting as if the people around us were nothing more than motion picture screens for our projections. At the same time, our egos would have us deny responsibility for our projections, and these projections become defenses against the reality of God.

Perceptions are corrected when we stop seeing value in interpreting or judging the behavior or motives of others. We learn to quiet the ego and to listen instead to the inner voice, which goes by many different names: Holy Spirit, the inner teacher, the voice of wisdom, intuition, or the guide that is within the heart. This inner voice has been given to us by God, to interpret all things based on love and joining. The result is that our perceptions are corrected and we begin to experience ourselves once again as love, joined as one with God and with one another.

Practical Principles

I have found the principles in the *Course* extremely practical in every aspect of my life. The principles are really universal and have been around, in one form or another, for centuries. I would like to share some of my favorite ones with you. Each can be used as a meditation by itself.

There are only two emotions, love or fear. How we perceive is a choice. Rather than seeing another person as angry and attacking us, let us view that person as either loving or fearful, giving us a call of help for love. Forgiveness is the key to happiness.

It is only our own thoughts that hurt us. It is only our own minds that need to be healed. We are not victims of the world that we see.

Let us make no judgments and relinquish any value we find in guilt or in holding on to grievances and blame. Let us let go of the temptation to interpret other people's behavior and step back to let God lead the way.

Let us choose love instead of fear. Let us choose peace instead of conflict. Let us remember that unconditional love has nothing to do with how we or anyone else performs.

Honesty is when all thoughts come from love, and when there is harmony in what we think, say, and do. It is where one thought does not oppose another. It is a state of mind where there is only peace.

Help me to have the same interest in another person as I have in my-
self, and to understand that God's will for me is perfect happiness. I do
have a right to be happy.

I will not be afraid of love today.

Lessons in Forgiveness

Through daily spiritual studies, I began learning how
to let go of my grievances. I started, perhaps for the
first time, to take responsibility for my life and for
everything I experienced. I also began to change my
lifelong belief that I was a victim of the world. Learning
the power of forgiveness allowed me to begin healing
old and sometimes bitter relationships that I had
thought could never be healed.

I began to see that it was not people or conditions in
the world that upset me; rather, I saw that my thoughts
were the cause of my upset. Light began to shine
within, bringing clarity that transcended what my eyes
saw. I began to understand that the world I perceive is
one I first create in my mind and then project onto the
external world.

As I continued on my spiritual path, I gradually experienced more and more peace and happiness, beyond
anything I had previously known. My mind began to
open to the fact that we are all equals in our lives,
equally teachers and students of one another.

Although my spiritual studies improved my life, I
continued to bump into old ego resistances. For exam-

ple, at one point I had lesson cards all around me—in the kitchen, in the bathroom, and in the car—but I still forgot the lessons for the day. In my daily studies I would catch myself reading the same paragraph over and over again, unable to understand the simple lessons given. There were days when I had convinced myself, once again, that I was mentally defective.

In July 1975 a small group of us in Tiburon, California, started a weekly meeting of students of the *Course*. This support was tremendously helpful as we struggled with our lessons. There are now a large number of groups that meet weekly all around the country. But the majority of students study the *Course* alone.

Although I dedicated each day to my spiritual path, I continued to drink. One part of my mind told me that my path could lead me out of my self-imposed imprisonment with alcohol, while another part said there was no escape from my addiction. For the first time in my life, I asked God for help. This was about four months after I began the *Course*.

I awakened about two-thirty in the morning, in a deep sweat and feeling very fearful. I was hearing a voice that seemed to come from outside me, rather than an inner voice. It was telling me that I no longer needed to drink. I was entering a new phase of healing. That statement was repeated three times.

I thought I was going crazy. Immediately I had visions of myself going into delirium tremens and seeing pink elephants on the walls. I was panicked and could not get back to sleep for over an hour.

Later that morning when I awakened I had success-
fully repressed the whole episode; I had no memory of
it. I went through my usual day's activities, and when I
returned home that evening I immediately reached for
my bottle of scotch, as I did every night. This time,
however, before I could pick up the bottle I heard the
same voice I had heard in the middle of the night. It
said, "You are in a new phase of healing and it is not
necessary for you to drink anymore." The statement
was repeated three times, just as before. I did not touch
the bottle.

It was hard for me to believe what was happening. I
had asked God for help every morning for several
weeks, but little had I known that help would come in
this form. I was amazed. It was like I was standing outside myself, looking at myself and not really believing
what was happening.

At this time my ego, with all its self-doubts, came
storming in. It told me that this would last only a few
hours, a day, or a few days at the most. My ego kept
saying that there was no way I could get rid of my guilt
and the most I could expect was to drown my guilt by
continuing to drink.

The rest of that night I didn't drink, nor did I experience any desire to. It was all happening without any
conscious effort. The next day, the next week, even the
next month, I had no desire for alcohol. To this day I
cannot understand why I never missed it.

In about four months I had lost thirty pounds. Until
then I hadn't been aware of how fat the drinking had

made me. What a joy it was the day I took all my clothes to the tailor to have the waists taken in! How grateful I was to God. I began to have some inner sense that with God's help nothing, absolutely nothing, was impossible.

> It is your thoughts alone
> that cause you pain.
> —*A Course in Miracles*

What could you want
that forgiveness cannot give?
Do you want peace? Forgiveness offers it.
Do you want happiness, a quiet mind,
a certainty of purpose,
and a sense of worth and beauty
that transcends the world?
Do you want care and safety,
and the warmth of sure protection always? Do you
want a quietness that cannot be disturbed,
a gentleness that never can be hurt,
a deep, abiding comfort,
and a rest so perfect it can never be upset? All
this forgiveness offers you.

> —*A Course in Miracles*

7

DEFENDING
AGAINST LOVE

Are the sounds in my head bothering you?
It is only my ego doing its dance.

Probably the most valuable lesson I learned during this period was how the ego operates, and how clever and deceptive it can be. It would have us believe that conflict, stress, attack, fear, guilt, and unhappiness are normal, healthy aspects of humankind. When it is most active, its dance is a series of dizzying moves, creating illusions that hide love from our awareness.

I began to see that there are times when my ego does what I call its "war dance," a dance for its own survival. The tempo of the dance increases the moment I begin to experience a sense of peace, because peace is the ego's enemy. And my ego does its war dance as a way of fighting God, because it is afraid that it will be replaced by God. Dr. Bill Thetford, who with Dr. Helen Schucman created *A Course in Miracles*, once jokingly told me that if there was ever a sequel to *A Course in Miracles*, it should probably be called *The Ego Strikes Back*.

All the ego's energy goes into defending against love. As long as I allowed my ego to keep me attached to doubt and uncertainty about love, it was able to maintain its rule over my life. My ego, with its belief in scarcity, taught me that there could never be enough love. And yet it did everything in its power to make me believe that I should be afraid of love, that love was untrustworthy and could hurt me. It told me to believe that thoughts of fear, attack, and defense would give me more security than the safety of love.

Those periods of my life when I listened only to my ego are best described by something I once heard Jean Houston say about this state of being: "We feel that we are merely layers of skin carrying around a dreary ego."

I began to see my ego as being made up of guilt and fear, working as a team to build a fence around spirit. As if spirit can ever be imprisoned! Whether it is really possible or not, I would have to be the first one to admit that my ego did a good job of imprisoning my spiritual being for years, convincing me that I was unforgivable. My ego fought against letting me recognize that walking over the bridges of forgiveness would free my spirit from my self-imposed prison.

The ego defends itself against love because it knows that when we truly awaken we will know that the ego's messages are illusions—and that love is the only reality there is.

The ego will do anything in its power to hide from our awareness the fact that our number-one problem in life is our fear of death and our fear of separation from God and one another.

I discovered that my fight with God was really a fight with my ego's resistance to love and its efforts to block my awareness of love's presence. Understanding that much was helpful, but the next step toward becoming free from the prison of the ego was the discovery that we can retrain our minds and change our perceptions of the world and ourselves.

The ego has its own rules, and as we come to recognize these we also begin to see the ego more clearly. It no longer has so many ways to hide from our awareness or manipulate us. And then we can start, with confidence, to choose whether we are going to listen to it or to the voice of God and love.

Sanity and the Ego

Imagine for a moment that we all have split minds: one part fully aware that we are love, another part fully convinced that each of us is only a body with a separate mind filled with fear and guilt. Surely this is not a model of sanity!

But what is sanity? As a psychiatrist, if I were to rewrite the *Psychiatric Nomenclature of Diagnostic Terms*, I would have only a single paragraph. I would define sanity as "that state of mind where there is wholeness, where all minds and hearts are joined as one, and where we are continuously giving and receiving the love we truly are."

Based on that definition, I have been insane most of my life, along with millions of other people. Until we know and accept that the essence of our beings is love, perhaps it would be better to consider that we are all equally insane, and that it is only the outward forms of our individual insanities that make us seem different from one another.

Defenses of the Ego

I will now list some of the ego principles that helped me begin to move out of my self-imposed prison and the circular dance the ego is based on. The defenses of the ego have only one purpose—to keep us in a revolving state of conflict, with a split mind that is afraid of love.

Our egos would have us think that many of the beliefs underlying the following statements are ingrained in our beings and can never be changed. But this is not the case. We can retrain our minds, and we can and do choose the thoughts we have.

Each of the following statements describes a message from the ego. These are the ways we begin to understand how the ego interferes with our experiencing ourselves as whole and loving beings. There is great temptation to believe in these statements, but keep in mind that they are all the ego's ways for hiding love and God from us. When we see these ego rules clearly, we need no longer be imprisoned by them.

The Ego's Defenses Against God

1. The purpose of a relationship is to find someone special who will love you more than anyone else. It is also to find out whom you can trust, and whom you can't.
2. The way to be happy in life is to think of yourself and your family first, to make a lot of money, and to have many material things and hang on to them.
3. One of the main purposes in life is to find someone you think you can almost love and then try to mold him or her into your idea of the perfect person.

4. When bodies die, that is the end of life.
5. Making others or yourself feel guilty is an important technique for making a better and more loving world.
6. Being demanding and getting your way is essential for a successful life.
7. To make it in life, getting is by far more important than giving.
8. Manipulating and controlling others are essential for success in life.
9. Love has boundaries and limitations and is limited to what we see and hear.
10. Measuring sticks are necessary for rating the relative value of each person's life and to know where we stand in comparison to other people. We must continue to measure others and ourselves endlessly, even if we kill one another by doing it.

Do we really have to believe that the past is going to predict the future? Do we really have to live our lives where the darkness of the past continues to cast shadows on the present? The ego would answer:

11. It is important to keep our past hurts and grievances alive so that we may know how to protect ourselves from being hurt in the future.
12. Attachments to people and things are healthy parts of human nature.
13. Be fearful of failure, but also be fearful of success.
14. Make all your decisions by yourself, based on your understandings and judgments of the past.

We become open-minded when we are willing to take a new look at all the values that we have been holding so close to our hearts.

15. Make idols of people and things and stake out your *ownership* of them.
16. Believe there is no God; or, if you must believe in God, believe in a vengeful, unforgiving one.
17. Be concerned about what other people think of you and always try to win everyone's approval.
18. Do not trust the goodness in people.
19. It is more important to experience stress than peace, because stress will make you feel more alive.
20. Accept the fact that for the remainder of your life you need to punish yourself and suffer because you have done things in the past that are sinful and unforgivable.

Is it possible that we may be ready to have faith and trust in a loving and forgiving God, and that we may be ready to step into Creation's footsteps by loving and forgiving everyone? No matter what our hearts might tell us, the ego will be sure to answer "no." There are a number of forms this "no" can take:

21. It is possible to experience total love and happiness and still have some people in your life whom you have not forgiven.
22. There are limits to the powers of the mind.
23. It is not possible to love everyone the same, and it is more important to love your blood relatives than to love people outside your family.
24. Keep a fence around your heart, and do not share your innermost feelings with others, because that knowledge will be used against you.
25. There are different kinds of love, and exclusive love is the best kind.

26. Helping and being of service to others is not as important as making sure that your own needs are met first.

The above statements are only a partial list of the ego's characteristics. The more we are willing to let go of our investment in these statements, the more peace and love we will experience. It may be helpful to review these statements from time to time, so that we may decide if we want to give allegiance to them and teach fear, or if we want to let go of them and teach love.

these statements... from time to time, sorted... may be...

CHAPTER

8

ATTACHMENTS

The way of the ego
is to have us forget about God
by getting and attaching ourselves
to people and things.

The way of Spirit is to have us
remember God by having no attachments
and giving our Love
to everyone unconditionally.

The ego wants everything and more, and it is never satisfied. No matter how much more the ego gets, it is never enough. Its goals are many, and they are always shifting. Our egos would have us attach ourselves to people and objects, holding out the hope for happiness. Many of us spend our lives going from one person to another, one object to another, frantically thinking that this will bring us peace and happiness.

Our attachments seem endless. And unless we are on guard, the minute we let go of one attachment another will take its place. We become attached to bodies and to specific parts of bodies; we become attached to sex, to our intellects, to our homes, to money, to objects of all kinds; we even become attached to fear, to thoughts of attack and defense, to anger and hate, and to worry.

Once I learned that I had a choice about what I put in my mind, I began to let go of my attachment to worry. The process of letting go unfolded from my understanding that I really did have a choice.

As we attach ourselves to people and things, our

egos have us make idols of them. These idols of attachment serve as defenses against our experiencing peace of mind. Our egos fight with God by having us cherish our attachments, by having us cling to the belief that there is always someone or something that we must have to make us happy and fill the void we feel. Our egos do not want us to believe that these attachments are only hollow substitutes for love.

With a world that is so attached to drugs, I would agree with Mother Teresa when she says that drug addicts are suffering from lack of love. What they need is more love, not more attachments or substitutes for love.

One of the best ways that I know for keeping God out of our lives is to be attached to money and make it our god. Yet, for so many of us, money is the number-one attachment. In this chapter I will share with you how I used my attachment to money to keep God out of my life and some of the things I found helpful in beginning to free myself of that attachment.

Guilt, Money, and Manipulation

When I started my private psychiatric practice in 1956, I made more money than I had ever dreamed possible. And I spent more money than I had ever dreamed of spending. And I *owed* more money than I had ever dreamed of owing!

I was a terrible money manager. I ended up living over my head, and, like my parents, I worried about money almost constantly. My ego and my attachment to guilt convinced me that I wasn't worthy of having money and the things it could buy. I ended up with a feeling of scarcity no matter how much I had.

As a husband and a parent, I was not above using money to manipulate other people. I always tried to control others, using money as my major tool. With my heart closed, filled with fear and guilt rather than love, I used money as a substitute for love, even though there was something inside me that knew it was not going to work. As long as I made money my idol, the awareness of the presence of God was nowhere to be found.

Many men control their wives through money, and many women are dependent and helpless, giving up their power in exchange for money and security. Many couples stay together only because of the husband's money. He makes all the decisions, keeping his wife on an allowance and in the dark about their financial status. Such marriages are built on control and fear rather than love.

During my divorce, the issue of how the money would be split became the number-one ego battle of my life. It is still painful for me to look back and see how fearful and insane I was.

When you are motivated to think of yourself first, when you are preoccupied with getting and holding on to things, there is very little peace of mind. Fear and greed are at the core of the ego, which always operates as if there is a serious shortage of everything.

To Give and to Receive Are One

The Center for Attitudinal Healing has offered me and others rich and bountiful learning experiences. One of the very important experiences I have had there involved my attitudes toward money and scarcity. In telling that story I hope that I will be able to share with others the process that led me to this healing.

My guidance was never to charge a fee for services at the center and to trust that God would provide. The philosophy of the center is based on giving, not getting. It gives new life to the principle that giving and receiving are, in truth, the same.

It is amazing how quickly our hearts open up to the presence of peace when we focus all our energy on helping a fellow traveler on the path. Today, the highest joy I experience has nothing to do with what I own or what I am going to get. It has nothing to do with money or the desires of the physical body.

For me, the most beautiful joy in the world occurs the moment I lose my concern about myself and my desires, and give a helping hand and my unconditional love and peace to another person.

One day, in meditation I received an inner message not only to continue to volunteer my services at the center but also to stop charging for services in my private practice.

Once again my fight with God was triggered, bringing up old messages of scarcity from my ego: How was I going to make a living? Who was going to pay my bills? Was this some crazy inner voice that I was hearing? Was I now entering some kind of spiritual psychosis? My ego kept telling me how stupid and ridiculous this was, and it suggested quite clearly that I forget God's plan and go back to writing my own script. My ego's trump card was that everyone I knew would think I was crazy, and hadn't I suffered enough of that sort of thing during my life?

To my utter astonishment, I followed my inner voice and chose to pay no attention to my ego. The process itself was easy: I made a decision not to worry about what other people thought of me, which was rare for me. Those of my patients who could well afford my fees were more than a little confused—but no more than I was.

Some months after I stopped charging for my services, my secretary talked to me about all the bills that were piling up. I had committed my entire life savings to my belief that I should not charge for my services, and I had already gone through my entire financial reserve. In a carefully diplomatic way, my secretary suggested that I needed psychiatric help.

Then some amazing things happened. I had been working on my book *Love Is Letting Go of Fear*. I knew that the writing was therapeutic for me but I had never expected the book to sell very well. That limitation turned out to be quite wrong, as did so many of my ego's judgments. The book became a runaway bestseller and an income was generated.

With the success of the book, I was asked to give talks all over the country. I had always considered myself as shy and clumsy, and the thought of speaking before an audience frightened me. Then, almost overnight, I found myself on the lecture circuit. Realizing that the voice of my ego was at the root of the fear and separation I felt over these lectures, I chose to stop listening to it and to start listening instead to the voice of love. And suddenly I wasn't afraid of lecturing to an audience anymore. I was actually enjoying it. As my ego gradually got out of the way, I stopped giving prepared lectures, as I'd done in the past. My ego was now starting to get out of the way, and I began to let the voice of love speak through me.

When I did this, people seemed to derive greater benefit from my talks. It was as if I was no longer doing the work myself. The words just seemed to be coming through me.

Money began coming in from the lectures and I continued to see people in my practice without charge. It was hard to comprehend that all this was happening. My old worries about money began to fade. In one sense, money began to appear to me as energy. It really wasn't mine; rather, it was an energy that belonged to God, an energy to be used for good.

Staying in the Present

Some years later, when I was visiting my son Lee at his home in Mexico, I learned an important lesson. We went to a very small market. Lee did something that day that I had never seen anyone else do: he bought one roll of toilet paper, one bar of soap, and one day's supply of salt and pepper.

When most of us go to the market, we buy a large quantity of these items, stocking up for the future. As I considered this, I remembered the words of Jesus when he said to have the trust of the birds who live in the present and gather only what they need for that day. It occurred to me then how much of my life I had been afraid of the future, and thereby had missed the present. And I also remembered the Peace Pilgrim, who gave up all her worldly possessions, having decided to live only in the present. She had absolute trust that God would always provide and never leave her comfortless.

I find my attitude about money is not yet consistent; it flip-flops from time to time. But for the most part I no longer worry about money or fear the insecurity of the future. Now money appears unexpectedly. For example, the center recently put on their first International Conference of Attitudinal Healing at the University of California at Santa Cruz. There were many who participated in the conference from around the world. The following week I received a parking ticket from the campus police. I sent them a check and forgot about the matter.

To my great surprise and delight, my check was returned to me. The letter accompanying it said: "I am returning your check of $12. I am very familiar with your book and feel that you must have been here to speak to a conference. I'm sure the money can much better be spent in your work with children." It was signed by the manager of the campus police.

In 1987 the People's Republic of China invited Diane Cirincione and me to bring children there through our organization, Children as Teachers of Peace. As the date for our departure drew near, money we needed to make the trip had still not materialized, and Diane and I began to wonder if the Peace Journey to China might not be in God's plan.

Then, at a lecture we gave, a stranger came up to us and asked about our trip to China. After we explained the situation, he asked how much money we needed. Six weeks later he sent us a check for exactly that amount.

A similar thing happened for a project in which we were helping war orphans in Nicaragua. A friend of ours in Europe, hearing about the need, sent a check covering the expenses for a special Christmas party for the orphans.

I was in Nicaragua that Christmas Day and had brought gifts and clothing with me from children in the San Francisco Bay Area. I wanted to phone home from Managua, but this wasn't possible.

However, a CBS television news crew attended the party. They filmed it all, including me in a red Santa Claus suit giving out presents. Many of my friends and family saw the news that night, so I didn't have to make that phone call back home. I like to think that I was being blessed by God that day and that celestial arrangements had been made for me to communicate with my loved ones in the States.

Before I made a decision to follow a spiritual path, things like this never happened to me. Yet, today they happen with greater and greater frequency, and I am learning that miracles are a natural occurrence.

On my 1978 Honda Civic, I have a bumper sticker that says: EXPECT A MIRACLE. I do.

I believe there is only one attachment that can save and bring peace to the world, and that is the attachment of giving unconditional love to one another.

With True Love
   there is always
      a childlike sense of wonder and
        an appreciation for
          the mystery of life
            that is beyond our human
              comprehension.

CHAPTER
9

FINDING A SENSE
OF PURPOSE

LETTING GO

Help me to let go of my preoccupations
   with the future.
Give me the strength to stop
   my futile attempts
   to predict and control the future.
Let me see no value in my plan
   of what the future should be.

Rid me of my senseless questions
   about tomorrow
And of all my desires to manipulate
   and control others.

Remind me that my fears and uncertainties
   of tomorrow are only related to
   my unfounded fear of You.

Help me be still,
   help me listen and love.

Awaken me to the truth of Your Presence
   being only in the now of this moment.
Lift me up into Your Arms and
   remind me that I am Your Creation,
   and that I am the Perfection of Love.
Help me to acknowledge that I am Your Messenger
   of Love, and free me to shine
   Your Light everywhere.

Let me feel Your Freedom within me, and
   let me laugh at the illusions
   that my ego once made
   me feel were so real.
Let me be light; let me be joy; let me know that I am
   the reflection of You wherever I am,
   and wherever I go.

The ego does not want us to know that its purpose is to keep us embroiled in fear, with a belief that there will always be separation and suffering in the world. One way it does this is by having us constantly judge other people, deciding who is guilty and who is deserving of our attacks.

I am still appalled at how often I allowed my ego to run rampant, and how much time I spent feeling that my purpose in life was to be a faultfinder and a judge of other people's behavior. In one sense, without being aware of it, I acted like the same vengeful god I feared, deciding who was guilty, who was innocent, and who deserved my love. My psychiatrist's credentials gave me credibility for doing this with professional dispatch, both inside and outside my office.

Before 1975, I wasn't aware of how much of a fault-finder and critic I was. One horrendous example of this involved my answering service. I felt so ashamed of this episode that for a long time I didn't share it with anyone.

I am the only physician I know of who was ever fired by his answering service. There have been plenty of physicians who have fired their answering services, not the other way around. At the time, I was having all kinds of problems with my service; they would forget to give me messages, or they would give me wrong telephone numbers. It was terribly frustrating and I complained a lot. I felt most righteous and was certain my anger was fully justified and that each complaint was valid.

When things went wrong, I was not the least bit hesitant to give the service operator a piece of my mind, letting whoever was on duty at the time know exactly how I felt. Despite my complaints, however, the problems continued and my anger and resentment increased.

You can imagine my surprise when I received a letter stating that because I was so hard to get along with the answering service was no longer going to do business with me. I told myself that all physicians had trouble with their answering services from time to time; I was sure I was no more complaining or cantankerous than anyone else. I was dead wrong. I was told that I was the most difficult customer that service had ever had.

That was certainly not the picture I had of myself. I wanted to believe that I really was a nice guy, who was no more angry than any other physician who used the service.

As I forced myself to look at the situation I had created, I began to see a lot that I did not want to see.

I began to see how abrupt I could be with people on the phone, especially the operators at the answering service. I put myself in the operators' shoes and began to understand their impatience and hostility toward me. I asked myself how I could be kind, patient, and loving to those who came to see me as patients while I could be so cruel and attacking to others. It was very painful to see myself as others saw me.

After starting the Center for Attitudinal Healing, one principle that became very important to us was: "This instant is the only time there is." As I worked with this idea, I began to see how, on the phone, I talked quickly so that I could get on to the next piece of business, which always seemed so much more important than whatever I was doing at the moment. I was still so absorbed in the future and the past that I didn't feel I had time to be forgiving and loving in the present.

I became more conscious that whatever moment I was in was the only time there was, an eternal moment for loving, for forgiving, and for giving. I did my best to see that the purpose of every relationship is to *join*. I also began to remind myself that God is never in a hurry.

I went to a new answering service and brought a completely new attitude along with me. I wanted to heal my past by forgiving myself and letting go of my old loyalty to my ego. I was clear that my purpose in all relationships was to join, to give, and to love. A few minutes before calling my new answering service, I would offer a little prayer, asking for God's help to be loving and forgiving regardless of the problems that might occur. I reminded myself each time that there was no moment in life more important than the present one.

I told myself that my purpose in life was not to *get* and not to judge others. I kept telling myself, over and over again, that my purpose in life was to be loving and to extend my inner peace.

This was by no means easy for me. My previous patterns of behavior were so automatic that if I didn't stop and think first, I still judged and dumped my anger on other people.

Then an amazing thing began to happen. I found myself much more peaceful on the phone. I was no longer in such a hurry. It became exceedingly important to remember that at this very moment I could be at home in the heart of God. The future was really right now.

Finally, it dawned on me that I would never be able to extend and give love to others until I was willing to accept God's unconditional love for me. As long as I saw the world as a hostile, unloving place, I could never truly be gentle with others.

It has been difficult for me to let go of the belief that I was not deserving of love because of my guilty past. But slowly I began to change my belief system, and what I perceived as a "miracle of love" occurred:

Some months after hiring the new answering service, I received a call from the company's owner, telling me how much they enjoyed working with me and how much they admired the work we were doing at the center. They said they had made a decision to give free answering services to the center indefinitely.

I am learning that there are always witnesses to the

truths that come into our lives to remind us that we are on the right path.

The peace of mind that I experience is exactly proportionate to how clearly I keep focused on my purpose. Yet, there are still some days when that purpose seems quite foggy to me.

10

THE BEGINNING OF SURRENDER

I felt the light within me today.
I felt the power of God's Love
Like a gently rushing river
Going through every aspect
Of my being . . .

What happened? What did I do?
I simply stepped back,
Put my ego aside,
And let God lead the way.

My surrender to God began when I finally realized that my old way of making decisions was simply not working. It did not bring me peace and happiness.

I had begun to recognize that in making decisions based on my ego, I was choosing to suffer and to play the role of victim. The more I forgave others and myself, the more I was able to let go of my need to suffer and sacrifice. The ego would hide from our awareness the fact that none of us need suffer unless, on some level of consciousness, we have chosen to do so. It is not other people or events that make us suffer.

Coming to God with Empty Hands

Perhaps one of the most difficult lessons for me has been that of surrendering to love and to God. The process has been presented to me in so many ways, from the lesson I was given when I stopped charging money for my services, to the time that I realized I no longer had to prepare my lectures, to the time I began changing my attitude with my answering service.

Whenever I backslide and my ego starts pushing to

be heard, I remind myself that all I have to do is be willing to stop trying to write my own script. Slowly, I am learning to let the Creative Source of the universe be my director and scriptwriter. How difficult it often seems, and yet how easy and liberating it really is when at last you come to God with empty hands to say, and really mean: "Let your will and mine be one."

In September 1975 I began taking photographs of people's open hands. In the stairway of my home is an entire wall of photographs of open hands. They are there as my daily reminders that if I want to experience the peace of God and allow him to be the director of my life, I must hold onto nothing and come with empty hands.

I began to realize that in spite of all my expertise in psychiatry, I didn't know what was best for me, let alone what was best for anyone else. When I began to listen to the inner voice of wisdom, rather than to my ego with its millions of misperceptions that I had once called "facts," a whole new reality, filled with hope, opened up for me.

I find that when I wish to be still and to listen to my inner guidance, it is necessary, if tedious, to empty my mind of conflicting thoughts. A process that I sometimes find helpful is to create a mental image of a garbage disposal. I visualize myself dumping all my conflicting thoughts into it; then I throw the switch to get rid of all my "garbage" thoughts. It usually doesn't take long for God's loving thoughts to replace all those negative ones.

❦

A person I admired and who was a valuable teacher to me and thousands of others was the Peace Pilgrim. When she reached old age, she received inner guidance to give up all her worldly possessions and to be a peace messenger, led only by the voice of God. She never knew where she was going to sleep each night or where her food would come from. She told everyone that she simply trusted.

I saw her on television shortly before she died. One could see that the interviewer was deeply impressed by her presence. He finally said to her, "You radiate such amazing peace and joy. What is your secret?" Her quick and simple response: "I don't have any junk thoughts. And I don't eat any junk food." There was no doubt that she was letting God write the script of her life, every moment of every day. Her trust and faith were not partial; she gave herself to them 100 percent.

I have often thought what a better place the world would be if we all followed the inner path of the Peace Pilgrim.

It requires humility to trust our inner voice. When I started studying the *Course*, I trusted only the voice of my ego; the word *humility* wasn't even in my vocabulary. My ego continued to remind me that I had all those college degrees; surely my education and my past experiences were more trustworthy than that inner voice, which I was not even certain I was hearing.

Although I feel increasingly certain that I am following the right map and am going in the right direction—listening, being still, surrendering, and learning to trust—my trust in my inner guidance continues to be one of my major struggles.

People on the Path

Robert Young

Robert Young and his wife, Betty, have been dear friends and supporters of the Center for Attitudinal Healing in Tiburon for many years.

Bob once shared with me that when he was in the television series *Father Knows Best*, his teenage daughter asked him, "Dad, how come each week on television you solve the most difficult family problems imaginable, and yet at home you seem so stupid?" He laughed and replied, "Well, honey, at the studio I just have a good scriptwriter." I have been fortunate to be witness to Betty and Bob, a most devoted couple, doing their best to follow their spiritual path and let God be their scriptwriter. And that is what surrender is all about.

Most of us go through life stubbornly writing our own scripts or allowing other people to write them for us. It is difficult to accept the possibility that in doing so we are living our lives based on very fragmented perceptions of the past. We rarely see things as they really are, and we almost never see things whole. That is why each person's perception of the same event always seems so different, telling us more about each person's ego than about the truth. We continue to see what we believe.

The form each person's ego takes is quite different, but the core is always the same. Because our egos are, above all, defense mechanisms, they know only how to write scripts based on fear. Our egos know only how to make decisions based on our past experiences, always thinking of ourselves first. They tell us to protect ourselves from the future by making decisions based on past judgments and old wounds. The ego's motto is: "Don't trust in love. Don't trust in God. And don't ever surrender to God or anyone else."

Mother Teresa

Although I have told it many times in the past, there's a story about surrender that is worthy of repeating here.

I have been most fortunate to spend time with Mother Teresa on several occasions. The first time we met was in Los Angeles in 1979. At that time she asked me why I had come to see her, and I replied that I wanted to learn how to surrender totally to God. For me, Mother Teresa, perhaps more than anyone else in the world, represented someone who has learned to do this.

We talked about many things during the first hour we were together. I don't know when I have ever experienced greater peace of mind. She was scheduled to fly to Mexico City later that day, and I wanted to go with her but felt afraid to ask.

Finally I mustered up my courage and said, "I'm feeling so much peace just being in your presence. Would it be possible for me to fly with you to Mexico City, just to be in your presence and to pray with you?"

Her reply absolutely delighted me: "Dr. Jampolsky, I would have no objection if you wanted to come with me to Mexico City." And then slowly, gently, and lovingly she added, "But I thought you came to see me to learn something about total surrender."

"Yes, Mother, that's exactly why I'm here."

"Well," Mother Teresa continued, "I think you can learn more about total surrender by *not* going to Mexico City with me and giving the money that you would have spent on that trip to the poor."

I flew home to Tiburon and sent checks for the price of a round-trip ticket to Mexico City and to Brother Jeremy at the Brothers of Charity in Los Angeles. Then I wrote a letter to Mother Teresa in Calcutta, thanking her for her gift of advice. Six weeks later, I received a handwritten letter, several pages long, from Mother Teresa.

Each time I am with Mother Teresa we discuss the topic of surrender. Once she told me that we just can't pay attention to God every second of the day in our busy lives, but that the important thing is our *intention* to do so. In that one statement, a tremendous amount of guilt was wiped from my mind.

While on an international speaking tour with my son Lee, I encountered Mother Teresa once more; we were scheduled to speak at the same conference in Bombay. Lee and I had a car and were asked to drive Mother Teresa to the conference. Following the conference, she was scheduled for a lecture tour to three cities, and she invited Lee and me to join her.

We were traveling in the same car with Mother Teresa for more than twenty hours. At some point Lee asked her, "What are the two most important characteristics a person should have if he or she wants to work in the healing professions?" She replied, "Humility and meekness." I smiled because these were two values they had never mentioned in my medical school. And I doubt that they are taught in most medical schools today.

During that trip with Mother Teresa I recalled the first time we had met and my request to spend more time with her. In the miracle I had experienced that day, I had received the lesson that when you let go of something your ego thought you wanted, the gift may come back to you in many wonderful ways.

I recently had a lesson in humility on an airplane. Prior to that trip, and on five consecutive trips preceding it, flight attendants had told me that they were students of *A Course in Miracles* and had either read my books or heard my lectures and had received much help from them.

On this particular trip I was starting down the aisle when a stewardess stopped me and said, "Hello, Jerry!" I paused, waiting for her to tell me that she had read my books or attended one of my lectures. Instead, she smiled and pointed to my sleeve.

And then I remembered: I was wearing a sweater with my name monogrammed on the sleeve.

I felt that God was giving me a gentle lesson in humility, and I recalled Mother Teresa's remarks to my son about humility.

Surrendering to God and being directed by an inner

voice can happen at unexpected times and in unlikely places—even in a bar. Several months ago I was reading the *San Francisco Examiner* when a photograph of a man's face caught my attention. He was a sixty-seven-year-old black man with a smile that went from ear to ear. The light coming from his eyes was extraordinary.

From the newspaper story I learned that this man had been a longshoreman all his life and had retired at the age of sixty-five. He was an alcoholic, and he visited the same bar every day. One day he found that he was bored and decided to ask the universe for help, but he did not really expect an answer. However, he heard a little voice inside him saying that he should go out and buy a broom and a cart. There was no doubt in his mind that for the first time in his life he had heard God's voice. He was then instructed to spend each day sweeping the streets around Mission High School. He did just that, and he stopped drinking. He soon found that he had become a surrogate grandfather for many of the students, and the kids dearly loved him and his wonderful smile. After getting to know this man, no student would dare to throw trash in the street.

This man wasn't after recognition; he wanted only to do God's work. He said that he has never felt as peaceful and happy as he does now. He knows that his mission in life is to be a messenger of God's love, and that the form of his giving is to sweep the streets and to become friends with the students at Mission High School.

Although this man is not famous, I believe that what he is doing is every bit as important as Mother Teresa's work. I believe with all my heart that each of us plays a very significant role in God's plan, for the short time we are here on earth in a physical form.

Surrendering begins by asking the Higher Power what we can do in our lives to help bring love, joining, harmony, and joy into our world. Each time that we accept the love God has for us, each time we give our love to others and put a smile on another person's face, we have taken a giant step toward healing a world suffering from lack of love.

When we are surrendering, when we truly want to listen, we may find answers on the lips of those who are closest to us at that moment. The answer doesn't always come from an inner voice. In my work with children I am reminded of this simple truth again and again.

I have a wise eleven-year-old friend named Lalita Riggs, who wrote a beautiful statement for our book *Children as Teachers of Peace:* "Adults are children, too, because in every adult's heart, there is a child's life that will stay there for eternity. So please listen to children, because when you don't, it is like not listening to yourself."

SURRENDER

And I asked, "What is the secret of
        total surrender to God?"

        And I was told,
"The secret of surrender is simply
                to be.
The secret of surrender is simply
                not to think.
It is letting perception gently
    dissolve into the knowledge of Love,
    the land of no change,
    the Kingdom of God.
It is hearing the waves tenderly
    kiss the surf,
    becoming united, becoming one.
It is perception dissolving
    into knowledge of the perfect
    one-essence of God and Love.
The secret of surrender is simply
    to do nothing and to be."

11

LISTENING

Love is Listening
and
Listening is Love.

There has been much written about the art of listening to our inner teachers, and yet for most of us the process of learning how to do this remains vague. Part of the difficulty is that such listening involves an experience that is hard to define with words alone. A greater part of the difficulty is that it is not in the ego's best interest to learn these skills. Distinguishing the inner voice from the voice of the ego is at the root of our self-made battles with God, and the ego doesn't want to make it easy for us to listen to our hearts rather than our heads.

I feel that I arrived late on the spiritual pathway. When it comes to listening to one's inner voice, I am in the preschool class. With that as a preface, I will share with you some of my struggles with listening and attempt to explain what seems to work and what doesn't work for me.

I have to remind myself constantly that there are only two voices to hear. Depending on which voice I choose to listen to, I will either suffer or be happy. The decision is not always a conscious one, but the more conscious I make it, the easier it becomes to distinguish between the two voices.

To start the day with a conscious decision to be grateful, kind, gentle, and patient with others helps to still the mind of my ego. That is quite a change from my previous way of waking up each morning, when I spent my time making a mental list of all the things I believed I had to do that day. I find that when I devote the early morning hours to God, in silence, I become open to a peaceful and happy day. It is a wonderful time to clean out any residue of negative thoughts left over from the day before.

The evening is also an excellent time to let go of whatever fearful, attacking thoughts may have accumulated during the day. I find that one minute devoted completely to God is far more valuable than an hour spent with my eyes closed in meditation with an ambivalent mind filled with conflicting goals.

❦

There have been many times when I told myself I wanted peace of mind but really didn't mean it. The result was that I received only the static rumblings of the voice of my ego. Many times I ask my Higher Power a question and get no answer whatsoever. I think there must be many times when I simply ask the wrong question. And certainly there are times when I am afraid of hearing the answer I might get, so I unconsciously stop listening.

There are other times when I think that I know what I want, and with the arrogance of my ego I go through an act of checking in with God—when what I am really trying to do is to nudge God into agreeing with my desires. This, of course, doesn't have anything to do with listening. It is only the ego attempting to manipulate once again.

But when I am truly clear about wanting peace of mind, I sometimes get an inner thought or impression. Sometimes I see a mental picture of a street signal flashing a green light or a red light. Similarly, I have a friend who gets an itch on his right hand whenever the answer is "yes."

Only recently have I come to value the precious experience of a still mind. Much has been written about prayer and meditation and it seems that there are as many methods as there are people. I prefer the simple approach to quieting the mind. For example, I find it helpful to slowly breathe in and out a number of times and remind myself that I am breathing love and peace. Sometimes listening to a favorite piece of music helps to quiet my mind.

I remind myself that I don't know what is best for me but that my inner teacher does. I try to remember that making a decision alone, listening only to my ego, is an invitation to disaster.

One of the laws of the ego is to get rid of peace wherever it is found. With lightning speed, the ego can turn peace into turmoil, convincing you that you can't be fully alive unless you experience conflict and stress.

What helps me the most is when I remind myself that I want all of my communications to be based on love and joining, not on fear and separation.

I want my every thought, word, and action to be loving. My desire is to be a messenger of God, a messenger of love. And each day that I am tempted to make a judgment against someone, I know that I have forgotten my true desire and purpose. I know that the ego, with its fear state, has taken over.

Most of us, myself included, have learned to be better talkers than listeners. To listen to another person with total attention and patience, to listen with no attempts to interrupt, to listen with no condemning judgment, is what unconditional love is all about.

I once visited a hospice in New Zealand. A volunteer I met there wore a pin with her name on it, and a single word below her name explained everything about her: LISTENER. It was clear that she was not there to give advice or to make judgments. She was there to give unconditional love, to listen, and to know that listening is loving.

Asking for Help

One of the first times I witnessed the power of listening to the inner teacher was in the fall of 1975. I had been moved by what might have been passed off as a routine remark by an eight-year-old boy.

It is important to know that this event occurred very soon after I had begun to ask the universe what God wanted me to do with my life. It was a significant experience for me because, in his own way, the little boy helped reveal the answer to my question.

The boy had a serious cancer and he knew it. During the doctor's ward rounds, on which I was a visiting physician, he asked his doctor, "What is it like to die?" The doctor changed the subject.

I became curious and upon investigation discovered that changing the subject was not an unusual response to such questions. On further investigation, I discovered that children usually look for someone they can trust and who will give them honest replies to these questions. On one particular ward, this turned out to be the cleaning woman. The kids seemed to know that they would get honest, direct answers from her.

Shortly after this incident at the hospital, while I was on a flight home from New York City, I began thinking about the boy's question about death. Suddenly it occurred to me that children like him needed a safe haven to be heard and to talk about their concerns. Perhaps here was an area of unmet need where I could be helpful.

I am learning that when you ask for inner guidance and you truly want an answer, you must step aside and listen, for that answer will certainly come. During my flight home that day I received a long message, giving me a purpose and plan that completely changed my life. The information came to me almost like inner dictation.

The message included a vision for starting what is now called the Center for Attitudinal Healing. I was told to start an educational center that would supplement medical care, and it would be based on the spiritual principles of *A Course in Miracles*.

Initially the center was to see children who were facing life-threatening illnesses. Ironically, all this was coming into reality when I was drinking myself to death and was obsessed with the fear of dying. My guidance told me that these children would help me look at life and death differently. In helping them, I would learn not to be afraid either of life or of death. All services would be free. I was to volunteer my time. I was not to worry about money but was to trust that God would provide.

The Center for Attitudinal Healing, in Tiburon, California, was founded in the fall of 1975. Today we not only see children and adults who have catastrophic illnesses, but we provide training for those who wish to learn to apply attitudinal healing in their own lives.

In the children's groups, we see kids who are facing life-threatening diseases, along with their siblings and other family members. We also see children whose parents have catastrophic illnesses. We see both adults and children who have AIDS, and we have support groups for their lovers, friends, and families.

For many years we have had a telephone network, which I like to call the "Love Network." This network matches people who have similar problems, putting them in touch so that they can help one another.

Another large part of our work is our "Person to Person" program. Here we put together people who wish to practice the application of attitudinal healing principles, such as communicating without making judgments, practicing forgiveness, and refraining from giving advice.

The concepts of attitudinal healing are based on the belief that it is possible to choose peace rather than conflict, and love rather than fear, regardless of the situation you are facing.

Attitudinal healing is the process of learning to let go of painful, fearful attitudes. At the center, our definition of health is "inner peace," and healing is the process of letting go of fear. We believe that love is the most important healing force in the world. The principles we apply are equally valuable in learning to listen to the inner teacher.

There are twelve principles of attitudinal healing:*

1. The essence of our being is love.
2. Health is inner peace. Healing is letting go of fear.
3. Giving and receiving are the same.
4. We can let go of the past and of the future.
5. Now is the only time there is, and each instant is for giving and forgiving.
6. We can learn to love ourselves and others by forgiving rather than judging.
7. We can become love finders rather than faultfinders.
8. We can choose and direct ourselves to be peaceful inside regardless of what is happening outside.
9. We are students and teachers to each other.
10. We can focus on the whole of life rather than the fragments.

*Our center has put these principles on bookmarks. They are free, and if you wish to have one simply write to the Center for Attitudinal Healing, 19 Main Street, Tiburon, CA 94920. Please enclose a self-addressed stamped envelope.

11. Since love is eternal, death need not be viewed as fearful.
12. We can always perceive others as either extending love
or giving a call of help for love.

Other Centers

In 1976, while I was lecturing in London, a friend took
me to see a famous psychic named Ena Twig, who is
now deceased. She knew nothing about me. However,
she told me that the idea for the center I had just started
would spread and soon there would be similar centers
all around the world. At the time, I thought she was a
sweet old woman who didn't know what she was talking about.

To my amazement and delight, the reading has
turned out to be correct. There are now over forty Centers for Attitudinal Healing, located all around the
world. Had I heard that in my guidance back in 1975, it
likely would have scared me so much that I would
never have done anything at all! This experience and
others led me to believe that when we go into stillness
and listen to that inner voice, we are only given the
amount of information we need or can accept at the
time.

Where Do I Belong?

Every day I find new lessons in listening, and new resistance as well. An event that occurred in 1976 stands
out above the rest. It was a monumental test for me; I
had to choose whether to listen to the voice of my ratio-

nal mind, my common sense, the voice of my desire, or to listen to that quiet, calm voice in my heart.

I was planning to go to North Carolina to participate in a weekend workshop on *A Course in Miracles*. I was looking forward to this conference, since many friends whom I had not seen for a long time would be there. I was to leave on Saturday morning, and I already had my airplane tickets. However, to my great surprise, on the Wednesday before, during my early-morning meditation, I received the inner guidance that I was to turn in my tickets and stay at home.

My initial response was to pay no attention—that the message was just part of my craziness. I thought I knew what I wanted to do, and I was not about to listen to some "dumb" voice inside me. For the rest of that day, and again the next morning, the same message kept popping into my consciousness.

Finally I gave up and turned in my tickets. But I experienced no peace. Rather, my agitation only increased. I began to think that once again I had done something very stupid. That Friday night I was so angry with myself that I could hardly sleep. Listening to inner guidance and surrendering to God was supposed to bring peace, but that certainly wasn't happening. Once again I felt like throwing away the *Course* books.

Saturday morning, when I would have been on my way to North Carolina, I received a telephone call from an eleven-year-old boy named Greg, who had been coming to the center for a short time and had been having trouble handling his gut feelings about his leukemia.

On the phone Greg told me: "You know, I haven't been able to talk about my feelings about having leukemia and my thoughts about death. I was wondering if you might be free this weekend. Could you come up to my house so we could talk?"

With great delight, I replied: "Well, it just so happens that I am free. And I can be there as quickly as it takes to jump in my car and drive up."

It turned out to be one of the most beautiful days of my life. Greg was able to talk about things that he had never discussed with anyone before. He asked me penetrating questions about my belief system concerning death. Pandora's box opened for both of us. It was a day of healing and tears and laughter. I was so glad I had listened to my inner voice so that my time was available for Greg. That day I knew exactly where I was supposed to be. And I had renewed faith in my Higher Power, which obviously knew far better than I where I was supposed to be and how I was supposed to spend my time.

The frosting on the cake was that I had an opportunity to talk to Greg's parents in the relaxed atmosphere of their home. I also spoke with Greg's younger brother. It was a day of transformation for all of us.

As I returned home I reflected on the fact that had I listened to the voice of my ego, which was so certain it knew what was best for me, I would not have been home to receive Greg's call.

Repeated incidents like this have given me more courage and motivation to accept the fact that I don't know what I am supposed to do. These incidents remind me again and again how important it is to take time out to be still, to listen, to trust, and to stay in the present.

❧

Not long ago I had an experience that was a gentle reminder of how to be at peace. As I was driving along in my car, the rearview mirror suddenly broke off and fell to the floor. This had never happened to me before. I decided to pull off the road and meditate on that. What came into my mind was the following: "Stop looking backward. Stop being stuck in the past. Stay only in the present, and that's where you'll find peace of mind."

It made me think about how we spend so much of our lives worrying about the future or holding on to grievances or self-blame from the past. Will I have enough money to pay the bills? Why did I spend so much on our vacation trip last year? Will I ever have the kind of relationship I want? Will our kids do well in school? Will I get the promotion I want at work? If only I had been fortunate enough to have the parents I would really have liked to have!

The voice of the ego, telling us to worry about the future and hold on to old grievances and self-blame, can fool us into believing that we must listen to it or something terrible will happen. Soon we are so filled with the past and the future that we have no time for the present. We can even forget that there is a present.

We have only to stop and remind ourselves that we truly can *choose* to listen to the ego, and thus hold on to these thoughts, or we can choose to fill our minds with the inner voice of love. When we choose to listen to the voice of love, the present suddenly comes into focus and we feel the love that God has for us.

Letting God Lead the Way

In 1975 I had no roadmap for my life, and I was like a rudderless sailboat in rough seas. Since then, I have slowly been learning to listen to the stillness within me by meditating and praying more, so that my whole life can become a prayer.

I now feel that my sailboat has a rudder, and that God is guiding my hand on it, telling me in which direction to go. I now know that the moving force of my life—the wind in my sails—is the purity of love.

There are still days when I find myself in rough seas, but more often than not the seas are calm and I can enjoy the warmth of the loving, glowing sun.

THE INNER VOICE

How do I know when I hear Your Voice?
  How do I know that my ego
  is not masquerading in a costume
  to deceive me once again?

"You will feel the extension
        of My Love
            in the harmony of
            what you think,
            say and do.

You will see only value
        in listening to My Voice
            and having the single goal
                of peace of mind, peace of God.

You will experience the peace of this moment
        as you symbolically ride the crest
        of the wave, effortlessly,
            feeling no sense of time;

Looking neither backwards nor
        forwards,
            knowing that you are the essence
                of the wave, forever extending.

You will have the willingness
        to experience the knowledge of Love
            that all of your brothers,
                sisters and you and I
                are One Self."

CHAPTER 12

MY FATHER

When we completely trust
God's Love and Gentleness,
we will have no fear,
and then we can accept
and experience Love and
Gentleness within ourselves.

As my work at the center continued, it became clear to me that I could not have peace of mind until I cleaned up my grievances from the past. I found that it didn't matter whether they were big or small; any grievance, of any size, was an obstacle to my experiencing peace in the present and kept me engaged in my self-created fight with God.

We teach what we want to learn. In 1976 I decided to make up a prescription for inner peace as if it were a physician's prescription. I put forgiving our parents at the top of the list, because we can't experience perfect peace, or give our peace and love to anyone, if we are holding onto these basic grievances.

At the time that I wrote this prescription, I still to some degree blamed my parents for my unhappiness and for my personality traits that had made my life difficult.

The truth is that our parents, no matter what our childhoods were like, did the very best they could. If we had had the same experiences they had while growing up, we likely would behave just as they did.

Let me share with you my father, Leo Jampolsky. He was born on a small farm in Russia in 1891, and he came to this country as a teenager. He used to tell me he was one of the world's first "draft dodgers." He moved slowly, and he was a man of few words. There was an inner gentleness about him, and although he had a temper he rarely showed it.

During the years I was growing up, my father worked from early morning until late at night. He was completely devoted to providing his kids with all the advantages he never enjoyed. I considered him a workaholic. He seemed afraid to make decisions; yet I now realize he took many risks in his life.

I remember wishing that he was more like other kids' fathers, who always seemed strong, decisive, and unafraid. As I grew into adulthood, I blamed him for my difficulties because I felt I had identified with his worst characteristics and had turned out to be just like him.

On the other hand, everyone in the neighborhood where I grew up thought of my father as a gentle soul. He had very kind eyes, and he always had a warm greeting for everyone. He loved baseball, and he loved taking me to games with him.

Although Dad usually gave in to my mother, there was, as in most families, frequent conflict around decision making. There were times when I blamed myself for these conflicts. At such times, I tried to play peacemaker, but experienced no success in that.

As an example of my parents' difficulty with communicating directly with each other, I remember that when my brother Les was away in Switzerland, getting his Ph.D., he would ask for money, which my mother didn't want to send him. Without her knowing it, my Dad would take money out of the cash drawer so that he could send it to my brother.

Early in my childhood, I took my father's side and blamed Mom for their conflicts. I frequently felt sorry for Dad. He worked hard in his store, but he seemed to have no power in his personal life. It was as if he had missed most of life, had just let it slip by him. I remember being very surprised when he told me that he had wanted to be a concert violinist. Of course, he had never pursued that dream, and in fact, as far as I know, he never took a single music lesson.

My father almost never talked about his feelings. At home he spent most of his time listening to the radio, which left little space for talking.

In my recollections of my Dad, I also have many wonderful memories of our family together, and I know that he was a caring and affectionate person, and that he did a great deal to create many wonderful moments. Frequently, on Friday nights, we all went fishing together, and in the summers we went on camping trips and got away from the city. When I think back on these times, I realize that there was a lot of love expressed in them.

I remember that as a child, everything I did seemed to go wrong. Being hyperactive, dyslexic, and physically clumsy, I must have driven everyone around me half crazy. In those days, no one understood hyperactivity and dyslexia as they do today, and I am certain that my parents were as bewildered about my behavior as I was. It must have seemed to them that because of my problems, I would never be able to fulfill the dreams they had for me.

My father listened to radio news broadcasts most of the day and night, regardless of whatever else he was doing. I think he listened to them to get away from his own fearful thoughts. I never knew what was going on inside him. Most of the time, he provided the maternal, nurturing qualities in the family. When I was young there were many times when I liked these qualities in my father, but at other times I considered them weak. It was years before I discovered that true strength comes from gentleness.

My parents kept a leather strap in the kitchen closet for what they considered major offenses. Mom acted as the judge, setting the sentence. It was Dad's job to apply the strap. That didn't happen too often.

I became a conforming, obedient, depressed, shy, resentful kid. Like my Father, I kept my feelings hidden, fearful of intimacy. The unwritten law was to hide and camouflage your feelings. It is hard to find intimacy when it is not safe to share your feelings.

One traumatic childhood incident remains vivid in my memory even to this day. My father took me to a poultry store when I was about five years old. We went to the back of the store to watch the butcher kill the chicken we had just purchased. The man took an ax and chopped off the chicken's head, then threw the body into an open barrel. Blood splattered all over the place as the beheaded chicken continued to make noise, jumping up and down in the barrel for a few minutes.

It was a horrendous experience for me. I wanted to deny what I was seeing. I tried to hide my eyes. I simply didn't know what to do with my feelings, so I held them inside. But at night I had terrible nightmares. There have been many times in my life when I have identified with that chicken. During times of turmoil, when my ego goes wild, I literally feel like that chicken in the barrel, jumping around with its head cut off.

The Contradictions of My Father's Life

On Thursday nights my father went to wrestling matches and sometimes I went with him. I did not realize it then, but I can now see that the fights were a wonderful outlet for my father. I liked being with him on the nights he took me along, but I did not enjoy the wrestling matches, which to me were the epitome of cruelty.

Dad often opened himself to ridicule and put himself in the position of being the butt of jokes. I remember one incident in particular. The family had set out to visit a lion farm that my Dad had read about in the newspaper. We spent all day driving around Los Angeles looking for the farm. Finally we stopped and bought a newspaper, only to discover that the farm Dad had read about was located in Illinois. We all teased him unmercifully. As I grew up, I, too, was frequently the butt of jokes, the one whom it was easy for others to tease. I blamed my father for that.

Dad was proud that his three boys all went to college

and became doctors, but he was disappointed that no one wanted to take over his date shop, which he and my mother had spent their lives building. Every time I tried to get my father to discuss his feelings about this, he would change the subject or walk away from me.

In the last years of his life, my father expressed gratitude to whomever he was with. He was almost always smiling and humming. It was during these later years that I began to see my father's strengths and what a great and powerful teacher he had been for me in the areas of acceptance, patience, and gentleness. I had found these character traits lacking in myself, but I was finally able to learn through his example.

A couple of years before he died, at the age of ninety-two, my father unwittingly played a part in healing a conflict between my brother Art and me. Dad had been living with Art but was visiting me at my house for the weekend. Art and I decided to get in the shower with my Dad, to give him a shower and wash his hair.

Dad complained bitterly about having his hair washed. Suddenly we were aware that the roles were reversed: Dad was the child and we were the parents. My brother and I remembered the Saturday-night ritual when Dad would wash our hair while we complained bitterly.

Suddenly a joining took place between my brother and me. Jointly giving love and care to Dad as we bathed him gave us the opportunity to feel once again a sense of oneness, tenderness, and joining with each other. The lesson for me was that you never know when or where healing is going to occur.

Shared Silence

My father was never able to share in words what was in his heart. But I learned from him that words are not necessary for love and the joining of hearts to take place. Dad had fears of dying, but he didn't talk about them. He did like me to tell him stories of the many children with whom I had worked who had faced death and had been my teachers. I believe that these stories helped Dad to come to peace with his own dying and to begin to consider that death does not cause separation.

There was one humorous incident that happened about a year before Dad died that I would like to share with you. My father spent what I considered an excessive amount of time just staring into space. I thought I could make this a more fruitful time for him by teaching him to meditate.

After I asked him a few leading questions, we had a rather deep discussion about how he dealt with the thoughts in his mind and how he valued a still mind. He didn't know what the word *meditation* meant. But it was very clear that this was what he had been doing for a great many years. Dad taught me a thing or two that day about learning not to make assumptions.

We spent beautiful, quiet times with each other during his last months. Words were not necessary for either of us. There was no doubt about the tenderness and love we felt for each other. We both felt complete with each other before he died. It was therefore quite a shock to me when, about six months after his death, I had an emotional outpouring.

I was writing an article that included a section about

him, and suddenly tears were pouring down my face. I sobbed. I missed my father. There were still more feelings inside me that I had repressed. How grateful I was to feel that intimacy with him and to feel his very real presence. I now have no question that when I am praying for guidance, his presence is there, helping me all the time.

Trust in God

When my friend Hugh Prather asked me if I remembered any childhood experiences when I trusted and felt the presence of God, I recalled an incident with my father. I was about five years old and we had just come back from a Sunday drive. It was growing dark, and I had fallen asleep in the car.

Dad picked me up in his arms and carried me into the house to put me to bed. I opened my eyes just for one second as he carried me in. I remember smiling and having the following thought: "I feel safe in my father's arms. He loves me so. I will always feel safe in his arms." I closed my eyes and slipped back into a deep slumber.

I now see that this moment was symbolic of my relationship with God. Today, it seems as if I am attempting to recapture the innocence of the little child in me, full of trust, knowing that God loves me totally. I now experience the joy of returning God's love through my work at the center.

In looking back on childhood, it becomes clear how our split minds work, how one part remembers only the negative things from childhood, where our needs are not met and when we wished our parents had been different. Another part sees our experiences and our parents in a totally different light. As I look back, I now see my parents as extremely loving people who did their best in raising their children. They had their ego problems, just as we all do, but they really did do the best they knew how and they did a perfect job of raising their kids and teaching them about honesty, human decency, and the courage to overcome obstacles.

It has taken me a long time to accept the truth that as long as we wish things had been different with our parents, we continue to blame them for the hurts we think we have suffered in life. And as long as we hold on to those thoughts, peace of mind will never be ours.

Many of us project our childhood resentments onto a whole new cast of characters that come into our lives. In an attempt to solve the problems we had with our parents, we live out the drama over and over again with the people in our adult lives.

To find peace, it is necessary to go to the source of our problems. I believe that most of the problems we have, in both our personal and professional lives, stem from the fact that we have held onto unforgiving thoughts about our parents and about God.

If we could just stop in our tracks for one moment, perhaps we might recognize that there is no sin in God, no sin in our parents, and none in ourselves. We all make mistakes, but mistakes can be forgiven. We are not here to judge, but to forgive.

Perceptions of hurts need to be honored, not hidden

from consciousness. But, through forgiveness, we also need to let go of them. And it takes just one split second to do that.

We cannot be free as long as we are imprisoning ourselves, and our parents with our grievances. It is only through forgiveness that we can experience our own freedom and theirs as well.

When I let go of my attachments to the past, I see my parents as others must have seen them—as gentle people who worked hard, who strived to be loving and caring to others, honest, loyal, morally decent and kind, and persevering in life against great obstacles.

As I choose to let go of my ego, with its attachments to negative experiences of the past, I begin to feel the love my parents had for me. They overcame many problems from a very difficult past and taught their children that each person can make a difference if he's not afraid to work and if he's made a commitment to his goals.

I now know that my parents loved me with all their hearts and souls. They were absolutely the right parents for me, teaching me exactly the lessons I needed to learn. The shadows of the past are gone and now there is only light and love between us.

I feel my father's presence with me each day. In my mind he continues to teach me one of my most difficult lessons—the power of God's love that comes with being a gentle man.

CHAPTER

13

MY MOTHER

When the world becomes free of guilt,
only love and peace will exist.

Many times in my life I have wished that my mother had been more lenient and permissive, like my friends' mothers. As both a child and an adult I was great with the *if onlys: if only* Mom had loved me more; *if only* she had not been so fearful; *if only* . . . well, maybe life would not have been so difficult for me. The *if only* perception is a very dangerous one and is designed by the ego to keep us in a state of distress.

As an adult I became an expert at rationalization. Mentally, I did an admirable job of figuring out why my mother was the way she was. And in my head, I thought I was able to forgive her for what I had *perceived* as her wrongdoings. However, there was still a part of me that blamed my mother for many problems I continued to have. Most of my life I have been fearful that other women would be like my perception of my mother, that they would be critical and try to control me.

Although I seemed capable and even enjoyed many successes in helping my patients work out conflicts with their parents, I continued to feel stuck with my own. Part of me was still trying to please my Mom and trying to get her to stop putting guilt trips on me.

The mental gymnastics I went through to forgive my mother never reached my heart. In my head I forgave her but not in my heart. I never totally forgave her until I started on a spiritual pathway. Only then did I begin to experience the limitless magnitude of God's love and forgiveness.

All Things Are Lessons That God Would Have Us Learn

Through my struggle to forgive my parents, I began to understand that when we feel abandonment, rejection, attack, or lack of love from our parents, this may be a projection of our fear of God. It is also possible that our tendency to blame our parents and others, or to become obsessed with self-blame and guilt, is a camouflage of guilty feelings that we are having because we have separated ourselves from our Source.

Today it is clear to me that every experience I have had in life, although it did not appear so at the time, was the perfect learning experience I needed. I am now grateful for every aspect of my life. Although I would not prescribe my own experiences for others, I do feel that I have been made stronger because of them. I now know that it is possible to take every experience that we have had with our parents, no matter what it was, and turn it into a positive learning for our lives.

Today, if I were to do it over, I would not change a single thing in my life. In one sense, I believe that we do choose our parents, and they teach us the exact lessons we need on our journeys. At this point in my life, I have nothing but love and gratitude in my heart for all my parents' teachings.

I am also very grateful for the lessons in *A Course in Miracles* that helped me change my perceptions and see my mother differently. Equally important, I am grateful for its lessons in helping me to see with humor things that once seemed so serious and painful.

My mother, Tillie Feldman Jampolsky, was born in England; her parents had migrated there from Russia. As I write these words, my mother is ninety-seven years old. I sometimes feel that she has lived so long because she had so many more things to teach me.

My mother was five feet two inches tall, but in my eyes she has always seemed about ten feet tall.

As a child I never questioned who was the boss in our family. It was my impression that my mother made all decisions and I never dared cross her. We never got away with anything. As a kid, I used to ask her how she knew what I was doing when she wasn't even in the room. She replied, "I have eyes in the back of my head." I learned to believe her.

My mother came from a most difficult background. She never really felt loved by her own mother, who died when my mother was a teenager. A few years before her mother's death, my mother's older brother told her that their mother hadn't loved her because she was adopted. My mother discovered that this was a lie only after her mother had died. She spent the rest of her life trusting no one.

One summer, when I was seventeen years old, I drove my folks from California to New York, where we visited every graveyard in Brooklyn, looking for my Mom's Mother's grave. My Mom had a strong desire to visit that grave, as though she had a plan for making peace with her mother. It was very, very sad because we were never able to find the grave. I don't believe that my Mom ever found the comfort she was seeking in her relationship with her mother.

Although Mom made all the decisions in the family, she didn't find those decisions easy. For example, when she bought clothes for herself, she was always unhappy with what she purchased and sent her selections back to the store.

I now see that my mother has had her own battle with God going on all her life. She didn't trust other people, she didn't trust God, and she didn't really trust herself.

Growing up as she did, it was difficult indeed for my mother to give love, for she still felt guilty and unworthy of love herself. Mom was both the most fearful person and the most overprotective mother I have known.

On hot summer days she had me wear sweaters for fear I would be in a draft and catch a cold. I fell into that belief system and I frequently developed colds after being in drafts. She was most tender and affectionate when I was sick, so naturally I learned to be a sickly, delicate kid.

It was not that my mother was not loving at other times. Like my grandmother, she was a great cook, and that was one of the ways she expressed her love. She was also convinced that being overly strict and controlling was a way to show love.

There was much fear and ambiguity in our house. Mom would frequently stop talking whenever I came into the room, which made me feel that she had deep, dark secrets about me. Her tongue was as sharp as her mind, and although she didn't intend to, she often made others feel guilty.

My mother was never happy with my becoming a psychiatrist. She always told me it was one of those "tricky" professions that tried to put all the blame on parents. She was convinced that people solved all of their problems by themselves, by "pulling themselves up by their own bootstraps." If going to a psychiatrist was a sign of weakness, becoming one was even worse. She would say that the whole field of psychiatry and psychology is a scam and a racket. The irony is that her interest in the radio talk shows, where people called in to get help with their problems, was one of the things that influenced me in choosing my profession.

She was no happier with my decision to follow a spiritual pathway than she was with my becoming a psychiatrist. In fact, she grew concerned about my sanity.

My mother was filled with contradictions. On one hand, she seemed rigid and set in her ways—unchangeable. On the other hand, she showed an amazing flexibility and a thirst for new knowledge. When I was a ship's surgeon for Matson Navigation Company, my Mom and Dad came to Wilmington, California to have lunch with me on the ship. It was a beautiful, calm day and this large luxury liner was tied securely to the dock. After being on the ship for five minutes, my Mom got seasick and had to leave.

I admire her so much, because two years later my Mom and Dad sailed on that same ship for Hawaii. And my Mom didn't get seasick even once.

Although my Mom had her own definite ways of looking at things, I was also impressed by her openness in taking in new information. For example, about five years ago, she became interested in discussing with me the possibilities of reincarnation. Another example: about ten years ago, I found out that she awakened at two o'clock every morning to listen to a radio talk show about sex. When I asked her about this, she smiled and said that she was learning a lot of new things that she never knew before, and then with a twinkle in her eye she went on to tell me that a ninety-one-year-old friend, who lived just down the hall from her, got married last week.

Mom liked my working with children and adults who were suffering from catastrophic illnesses, but she didn't like the fact that all my time at the center was volunteered. She was very concerned about my income. One day she said to me, "Jerry, listen to your mother. I am the only one who will tell you the truth. You are a fool going around the country talking about love, forgiveness, and God. Let religious people do that. Be a good doctor. Go back to your office practice and give pills to your patients. That's what physicians are for."

Pleasing Is Not Loving

Even as an adult I still tried to win my mother's approval, but she always seemed ten steps ahead of me. For example, in 1980, when she was eighty-nine years old and I was fifty-five, she asked me to get a new physician for her. I knew she had no respect for young doctors. To please her, and to avoid trouble, I chose a seasoned physician, someone my age. With great confidence I told her that I had found a new physician for her. As I had expected, her very first question was: "How old is he?" With even more confidence, I told her that he was fifty-five years old—the same age as I. "But I don't want a doctor *your* age—he's too young to know what he's doing!" she said.

Yes, Mom has taught me a great deal about patience.

❦

When I was finishing writing *Good-Bye to Guilt*, Mom asked me if it was another one of those books about forgiveness. I replied that it was. In all seriousness she said, "If you keep writing those books on forgiveness, I'm going to embarrass you and write a book about the importance of being *un*forgiving. People do things that are bad, and they should not be forgiven."

There was no debate. But I felt that, unconsciously, she was describing her own thoughts and feelings about herself.

She went on to say, "Everyone thinks I'm the most fearful person they've ever known, and you agree, don't you?" "Yes, Mom, you know that I do," I nodded. "Well, don't you see how wrong that makes you? I am ninety-two years of age and it is because of all my fear that I have lived so long. You are just going to have to go back and rewrite those books you have written."

Tenacity and stick-to-it-ness were in her blood. If there was a way to be found to make me feel guilty she would eventually find it. And very frequently I left myself wide open, obliging her like an obedient, good, submissive son.

One time I went to Whitehorse, Canada to lecture. Whitehorse is located way up in northern Canada. It is a most beautiful community. I phoned my Mom from the public phone booth at the airport, just to check in with her and see how things were going. Her first response was: "I don't believe for a moment that you are in Whitehorse, Canada. You are lying. I know that you are still in San Francisco." She went on to say, with the greatest confidence: "You are lying because you just don't want to visit your lonely Mother. What a rotten son you are!"

Then to top it off, she said, "I am going to prove you are lying. Give me the telephone number where you are calling from, and I'll call back and prove you're not there." I said, "Mom, this is a public telephone booth in Canada." She shouted, "Stop lying to me and just give me the number." I did as she told me, filled with curiosity about what was going to happen. Sure enough, a few minutes later the telephone rang. I heard my Mom's voice and I thought she heard mine. But before we could have a conversation, she hung up.

A week later when I visited Mom I gently brought up the subject of the phone call to Canada. I told her that I thought she had actually heard my voice and I asked what had happened. She promptly dismissed the whole matter by saying, "Well, of course I heard you. But I wasn't going to pay good money just to hear your voice." As it turned out, she had hung up the phone and complained to the operator that she couldn't hear me, in order to avoid paying for the call. Mom changed the subject.

Whenever I ran up against my Mom's hard edges, I had to remind myself of her many contradictions. Despite her scorn for psychology and psychiatry, she often tuned in to radio and TV call-in programs; she really was interested in how people could solve their problems. When my parents retired to Phoenix, she did volunteer work at a home for the aged. She enjoyed the work, and the people at the home valued her for her contribution. Whenever I put aside the judgments of my ego, I see her strong spiritual side much more clearly. I see that she has always been a deeply caring person.

Although I never knew exactly what it meant to her, I will always remember that when I was a boy she had a small statue of Gandhi. She and I have never discussed it, but I like to think that she was inspired by him and by his deep caring for his people.

Because my mother often put out the message that nothing was right, many people perceived her as a complaining, unhappy woman. She sometimes made guests feel guilty by telling them that they didn't visit often enough or long enough. Consequently, many people, including her grandchildren, cut down on their visits. In addition, she did not get along well with the head nurse at the nursing home where she now lives.

A few years ago I began to realize that if I was to have unconditional love for my mother, I would have to accept her choice to be unhappy, and that I could not allow myself to feel guilty or responsible for her in this decision. I began a practice of meditating for twenty minutes before each visit. As part of the meditation, I reminded myself that my job was not to please her but to love and accept her. This meant resisting my desire to change her in any way. It also meant letting go of the mold I had unconsciously created for her in my mind, the mold of the little old lady who was gentle, kind, happy, and loving.

I dropped all previous goals of trying to make her happy. It was now okay for her to be herself. My own peace of mind became my only goal.

After I began doing this, I discovered that I felt much more peaceful. My Mom didn't have to change at all. And yet, I no longer saw her behavior as an attack on me. I began to see Mom as a very frightened person. She was afraid of dying. She was afraid of losing control. She was afraid of not being able to give or receive love.

Some months after these changes, Mom asked me to bring her my audio tape series *Love Is Letting Go of Fear*. This request really surprised me. I brought in the tapes and she began to listen to them. Soon, the head nurse, with whom Mom had been in conflict, started listening to the tapes with her. To my surprise, they both began to agree with the principles on forgiveness, gentleness, and kindness.

In no time at all they were smiling and talking together. There had been a healing in their relationship. I like to think that they got through the fears and the attack thoughts that separated them and let their love for each other into their hearts.

The next week, Mom asked me and Diane Cirincione, my spiritual partner, to bring in some of the books I had written. She felt that they belonged on the nursing home's book cart—and that the people there could use some of "that stuff." She gave my books to a woman friend who had not talked to her sister in seven years; after reading the books, the woman forgave her sister and now they are talking to each other again. My mother laughed and said, "You know, this forgiveness stuff really does work." I was truly amazed.

Rather than complaining that we had not stayed long enough, she would look at the clock and tell us to go, saying that we must have other things to do. We witnessed the blossoming of gentleness and gratitude. Mom even began to use the word *love*.

Soon Mom began to kiss us on the lips instead of giving us her cheek to kiss. The first time this happened I was deeply moved. To me, it was proof that miracles really do happen, that with acceptance and forgiveness we do open ourselves to love.

I began to marvel at what happens when you stop

trying to change or please another person and let the love of God come into the relationship. How simple and how powerful!

I believe that my mother, in her nineties, experienced a spiritual transformation. My brother, whose belief system is quite different than mine, is convinced that my mother had a stroke. For me, she continues to teach that nothing is impossible, and that the power of unconditional love and gentleness has no limits. Old pains and scars have disappeared, and boundless gratitude and love have replaced them.

At Mom's ninety-sixth birthday party, she had the energy to blow out all her candles. She is as alert mentally as she always was, and she continues to do her job well—keeping all of us on our toes.

During a recent visit, I sat by my mother's bed for a long time and just held her hand. We didn't need words to express our love and to enjoy being joined, so for a long time neither one of us spoke. When it was time for me to leave, she smiled and said, "You know, Jerry, I not only love you, I like you!"

Forgiving Our Parents

I spend a lot of time with adults who are in the process of forgiving their parents. My own efforts in this area of my life have been invaluable in helping me to understand this process and encourage others in it.

Sometimes I put myself in my parents' shoes and I try to imagine that I grew up exactly as they did, learning about fear and love from their parents and from their environment. When I do this, I become much more empathetic with my Mom and Dad and I move one step closer to forgiving the things that seemed to go wrong in my own childhood, or that didn't turn out as I had wanted them to.

We learn to heal our relationships with our parents not by denying the hurt or anger we may feel but by letting ourselves experience and express those feelings. We do not need to express these things directly to our parents, but as we express them within ourselves, or in the safety of a spiritual or therapeutic setting, we can begin to recognize and take responsibility for our hurt and anger.

Forgiveness of our parents comes when we clear away the cobwebs in our minds, when we allow ourselves to see our anger and pain and then let go of it, knowing there is no value in maintaining our attachments to these feelings. When we let go of these attachments, love rushes into our hearts, and we can choose to say, "I want to let go of the anger and hurt that I feel my parents caused me. I want to ask for forgiveness and I want to love them totally."

Forgiveness is not a matter of feeling superior, of feeling sorry for our parents because they didn't know any better. It comes when we understand that as humans we all do the very best we can, and we can't ask for more than that. Forgiveness is making the choice to find no more value in anger, and to see that we are all God's light, all joined, and the separations we feel are only part of the illusions of the ego.

Forgiveness is letting go of the misperceptions that the ego would have us believe. We begin to have true peace of mind when we forgive our parents totally, when we let go of finding value in blaming them or blaming ourselves. We discover it when we let go of finding value in guilt. Peace of mind comes when we can perceive the world through our hearts and with our own bright, corrected vision, finding no separation, and finding that love is our only reality.

There is a wonderful quote from *A Course in Miracles:* "There is no order of difficulty in miracles." I didn't always believe that, but now I do.

> The nightmares of my life seem to disappear,
> as soon as I stop interpreting what I see,
> and let God do all the interpreting for me.

> I think that the most important
> Equation in the world is
> That the fullness of one's heart
> Is directly proportional to
> How much love one gives.

My Mom died in her sleep at 4:45 A.M., Saturday November 19, 1988. She had developed pneumonia two days before and when I visited her on Friday evening she seemed to be in a semicoma. I decided to spend the night at her bedside and felt blessed to be with her when she died. It was a very gentle and peaceful passing. She just quietly stopped breathing.

I don't think they make them like my Mom any more. She taught us all tenacity, never to give up, that nothing is impossible, and that you are never too old to change.

Mom always liked my brother Art and me to bring her pickled herring and cinnamon rolls. I have a hunch that it was the pickled herring that gave her such a long life.

In her last years she could not have been more loving and gentle to everyone, and in her last months, as her energy diminished, her vocabulary consisted of only five words, said over and over again. "I love you. Thank you." I can't help but think that if we all could live with only these five words in our minds and on our lips, it would bring much peace to each of us and to the world.

Mom was a tough and wonderful teacher to us all. I love her and miss her deeply. I feel most privileged to have been able to share her with you.

14

FROM SPECIAL TO HOLY RELATIONSHIPS

Tenderness and
   gentleness
Walk hand in hand

For where there
   is no fear
There is only Love . . .

And where there is only Love,
   there you will find tenderness
   and gentleness,
   side by side.

After 1975, my life focused on the people at the Center for Attitudinal Healing. I was also traveling, giving lectures and workshops on my books and on attitudinal healing. Day and night the center and its programs absorbed my being. It was not work—it was joy.

In addition to my other activities, I spent a great deal of time answering volumes of mail from people who had a wide variety of problems, and for many hours each day I responded to phone calls from people all over the world. I rationalized that I had no time for anything but the work, and even less time for close personal relationships. Although I did not want to recognize the fact at the time, it was not just my busy schedule but my fear that kept me from true closeness.

It is now very clear to me that even when you think you are on a spiritual pathway, you can use work as a defense against having to confront your thoughts and feelings.

Certainly "workaholism" is due in part to the fact that we are more interested in "doing" than "being." Because we fear intimacy, we choose to fill our lives with "doing," rather than allowing time to reflect on our most intimate thoughts. Howard Caesar, minister of the Unity Church of Christianity in Houston, recently pointed out to me that the word *intimacy* can be looked at as "in-to-me-see." It means letting another person see you as you really are.

I have found that there are many, like myself, who want intimacy but at the same time fear it. We are fearful that if another person sees us as we perceive ourselves, we will be rejected.

I had put aside the possibility of having close personal relationships, rationalizing that all of my past failures were signs that I was just not destined to enjoy human intimacy. I was to be absorbed in my work. Period.

No matter how good we are at convincing ourselves that we know exactly what we are doing and why, God has a way of tapping us on the shoulder to remind us that we are not writing our own scripts. Perhaps this is God's gentleness showing through, his awareness that his message might be too overwhelming if given straight on.

Diane Cirincione

My relationship with Diane Cirincione began months before I met her in person. One Sunday I opened my mailbox at home and found a letter someone had left there. The person had chosen not to sign it, which I thought was odd.

The writing was beautiful. It was on the subject of death and dying. I put the letter in my coat pocket and proceeded to drive to San Francisco, where I was scheduled to give a lecture on that very subject. In the middle of my talk, I decided to read the letter aloud, and it was very well received. I did not know that the person who had written it was in the audience. She had come to hear another speaker that day, not realizing I would be on the panel. She had no guidance to introduce herself to me that day, but later she said that she felt my reading her letter was a gentle sign that I would perhaps understand similar writing that was coming to her every day. It was several months after the lecture that I met that person—Diane Victoria Cirincione.

To me, Diane's writing was very much like that of Dr. Helen Schucman, who with Dr. William Thetford brought *A Course in Miracles* into being. The writing was like inner dictation. Diane's inner voice had told her that she was to meet me and to ask for my advice about her writing, but at first she decided to ignore that guidance.

Then, on August 20, 1981, as she was driving to her office, her car stopped dead right in front of the Center for Attitudinal Healing. Diane felt this incident was a strong sign that she was not to ignore her inner voice any longer. She walked towards my office and knocked on the door. We both experienced a jolt when I opened the door. I was talking with someone in my office at that moment, so I asked her to come back in about thirty minutes when I had a break.

When she returned, we spent about twenty minutes together. My heart skipped some beats that day. It was

6:45 A.M. and Diane, who had been on her way to her office to do some cleanup work, was dressed in grubby clothes. Yet there was a balance of outer and inner beauty and a gentleness that was beyond anything I had experienced before. I was so caught up by the quality of her presence that it was difficult for me to listen to her words. There was something breathtaking about the experience, an amazing sensation of an ancient familiarity—a feeling that we had met at another time, another place. It was like two souls coming together who had known each other many times before. My office seemed to light up with the energy between us.

We made an appointment to see each other in my office two weeks later. It was a difficult and chaotic period for me. The voice of my ego was incessant. I was well aware that the fence I had so carefully built around my heart had come down for a moment, and my ego wanted me to repair it and build it even higher.

My ego even went to the extent of using spirituality as a way of keeping me in bondage. My conversation with myself went something like this:

"You are finally on a spiritual pathway. The last thing you need is a new 'special relationship' with a beautiful woman who is twenty-one years your junior. You're just trying to recapture your youth. Stop your fantasies. If this relationship becomes romantic, it will lead you away from God. You're already having a tough enough time trying to find God. Don't add more obstacles."

When I tried to argue, my ego cut in:

"How many times do I have to tell you that you will

always be a failure with women? Close relationships have always failed, and they always will. You'll just end up getting hurt, and hurting her. She came to you for help with her writing, not to have a personal relationship. Forget about your loneliness. That is your destiny. Be objective and helpful when you see her. *But don't make any more appointments to see her.*"

There was another little voice within me saying that Diane was a gift from God and had come into my life to teach me that the way to go home to God was by having a close personal relationship become a holy relationship. All this inner chatter made me feel that I was losing my sanity.

The next time Diane and I got together, I tried to be objective and to keep an emotional distance from her, while inside I was petrified with fear. I wanted so much to do the right thing, and I did not want to fall into the hotbed of pain and misery again.

Having tried to be cool, distant, and objective, I was astonished to hear myself agreeing to see her again in my office, to talk about her spiritual writing on the evolution of consciousness of an individual soul.

Some months later I mustered the courage to invite Diane to lunch. It was quite a time. I did not realize what a powerful teacher she was going to be for me in the years ahead. When I automatically went to pay the bill, Diane gently stated that she would pay her share and that I should take a look at my assumptions.

Diane has continued to help me look at my assumptions about female/male relationships. I hadn't thought

I was holding onto any of my old male chauvinistic traits, but I was wrong. Many of them were still there, hiding from my awareness.

I found Diane's writings not only beautiful but extremely helpful to me personally. Until then, she had shared them with only two other people, but they were so uplifting that I asked her permission to read them in my lectures. She agreed, but only if I promised not to tell who had written them.

When I shared her sensitive writings with audiences, they were an outstanding success, and we received many, many requests for copies. At that time I encouraged Diane to publish her writings, but her guidance then, and for the next six years, was not to do so.

On the deepest level possible, from the very beginning, Diane and I have always felt a deep and tender soul connection. There was a bright gentle light in her eyes that went through me, from the top of my head to the tip of my toes. But there were many things on the surface that caused both of us conflicts. Once again my old feelings surfaced around how safe is it to trust. These feelings mingled with my unresolved feelings of jealousy and possessiveness, which I mistakenly believed I had worked out. Old films of mine began to run again. I learned that I had buried a lot of issues about personal relationships, rather than trying to work them out.

We both had guilt from previous personal and business relationships. There were many times that both of us had thoughts of going in opposite directions, of running away from each other.

One evening about two years into our relationship, I found myself becoming furious with Diane. She was not falling into the mold my mind had made for her. That can be translated into: Diane was not doing what I wanted her to do; she was not meeting my needs.

I began to interpret Diane's very healthy independence as a sign that she was rejecting me. I ignored all the spiritual principles I had been trying to apply to my life. In the heat of my anger, which I considered righteous and justified, I did everything I could think of to make her wrong and me right. Yes, I had chosen once again to be right, not happy.

I went to bed that night feeling enraged, bitter, and depressed. However, as my head hit the pillow, I had enough sanity left to ask God for help. I wanted peace of mind, not the inner agitation I was feeling. I was awakened at about 2:00 A.M. with a deep urge to write.

What came out was a meditation on friendship that I and many others have found helpful. It is now on a poster that also has a photograph of my parents holding hands when they were ninety years old. This writing has helped me look at friendship in an entirely different way.

Friendship

I thank you for teaching me what friendship is—a relationship that has no needs; where one's interest in the other person's welfare is the same as one's interest in oneself; that friendship is a state of mind, where

there is no fear, no guilt, no attack thoughts, no feelings of vulnerability;
where it is all right for you and others to see me as I really am; where
there is constant giving and forgiving; where the only desire is to be
helpful, gentle, and patient; where there is no past or future but only the
present; where each instant is for total loving and letting go and where
there is no holding on, no attachments, and no demands.

That friendship is a relationship where there is only light, only the
joining and sharing of love, and there is no exclusiveness; where the
geographical location and physical separation is of absolutely no impor-
tance; where there is complete and total love and acceptance regardless of
the illusory perceptions of separation made by time and space.

That friendship is eternal, a state where no thoughts, words, or deeds
can cause any feeling of hurt or separation, and where the light of Spirit
is the only reality.

That true friendship is a state of bliss, where we see only the God Self
in each other. It is a state of inner knowing that we are connected by Love,
with each other and God, forever.

I discovered that learning could come out of personal
conflicts, and that with God's help I could immediately
change my perceptions of a relationship, myself, and
the world. How grateful I was. With a shift in my perception, the basis for a whole new relationship with
Diane began.

It became very clear to both Diane and me that our
relationship would not work unless both of us committed ourselves to putting God first in our lives. We began to do our best to free ourselves of all attachments
and to "love and let go" each day. Prayer and meditation became daily essentials. Each day we made a sin-
cere effort to let go of our own plans and let God lead
the way. There are still plenty of times when we get

caught in the busy-ness of the day and we forget to be "still" and step aside. But we are learning that when this happens, we can take time to choose once again: Do we want peace or conflict?

With my past relationships, I always had a plan for the form the relationship was to take. I felt I needed assurance that the form of the relationship would stay the same. So it became quite a new experience for me not to prescribe what form this relationship should take.

In the spring of 1984 a dramatic shift took place between Diane and me. Just as I was about to give a lecture, I developed laryngitis. Some other members of the staff offered to fill in for me. I had planned to read some of Diane's prose, so I asked her if she would read it in my place. She immediately refused. When I asked her if she had prayed on that, she said "no." She then prayed and, to her surprise, got a "yes" answer.

Diane had been one of the most private people I had ever known. She had never spoken before a large audience. However, that night, it was as if she had been speaking publicly all her life. The healing light of love that she radiated affected everyone. It was not possible for her to ignore the wonderful feedback that she received from the audience.

We gradually began to lecture together, and our travels have taken us all over the world. Our most frequent talks and workshops are Attitudinal Healing; The Healing of Relationships; Love Is the Answer; and The Practical Applications of Attitudinal Healing Principles in AIDS.

There was one night that our personality selves showed their true colors. We were speaking at the Opera House in Seattle, Washington. The house was packed and we were behind the curtain, about to be introduced. I peeked out and saw the huge auditorium, completely filled with people. I got scared and told Diane that I was sorry, but I just had to go to the bathroom again. It was difficult finding the backstage bathroom. Afterwards, in trying to find the stage again, I made a wrong turn and got lost.

Meanwhile, Diane was developing her own fears; she was asking herself what she would do when the curtain went up and I was not there. This was when we had first started speaking together, and she was not that well known yet. That night she felt the people had come to hear me, not her.

Diane told me later that as the announcer was introducing us, she was becoming more frightened and furious, and she just wanted to kill me for leaving her there to face the crowd alone. She finally decided that if the curtain went up and I was not there, she would simply tell the truth—that I had gone to the bathroom at the last minute and had probably lost my way back. Just as the curtain started to go up, I came running breathlessly onto the stage.

I thank God Diane didn't have to give her explanation that night.

As we have worked together, doing our best to listen to our own individual guidance, we have noticed a greater balance in the male/female aspects in each of us. If there is a key to the success we have had in helping ourselves and others, it is that we make every effort to feel our own wholeness in relationship with our Creator.

There is a very significant prayer from *A Course in Miracles* that we have personalized and say before every meeting, lecture, or workshop that we conduct. It's a quick way to lay aside our egos, to let go of fear, and to let the light of God shine in us and tell us what we should think, say, and do. It goes like this:

> I am here only to be truly helpful.
> I am here to represent You Who sent me.
> I do not have to worry about what to say or what to
>   do, because You Who sent me will direct me.
> I am content to be wherever You wish, knowing You
>   go there with me.
> I will be healed as I let You teach me to heal.

Letting Go of "Specialness"

The belief system of the ego would have us think that we live in a world of scarcity and that some "special" person will come into our lives, sweep us off our feet, meet all our needs, love us more than anyone else, and stay with us forever, with the sole desire of making us happy, no matter what we do to them. When our relationships are based on the hollowness of the ego's illusions, it is no small wonder that so many of us have trouble sustaining intimate relationships.

Let us look a little more deeply at how the ego uses relationships to hide the presence of God. The message of the ego is that there is no God and no one can be trusted. So the ego is frequently running at full speed, trying to manipulate others, being concerned about the form of the relationship rather than its content. The ego thinks that relationships are to be owned, controlled, and put into molds of one's own liking.

When we follow our egos in our relationships, we initially develop the illusion of love. But the moment our needs are no longer being met, the honeymoon is over. A love-hate relationship develops as we become frustrated and angry about what we perceive to be our unmet needs.

Anger, blame, attack and defense, possessiveness, jealousy, control, deception, dishonesty, and withholding become the plan for the day. When we have all these ingredients cooking on our internal stove, God is once again pushed out of sight, nowhere to be found.

As I look at my past relationships, as well as at certain aspects of my relationship with Diane, I see with increasing clarity my ego's capacity for creating a fog so thick that I can no longer see God.

Diane and I have worked very hard to have our "special relationship" become a holy one. This means that we strive to devote our relationship to God rather than to us, doing our best to acknowledge and support each other's inner guidance. We still have our bumps and crises; we make mistakes and fall down. But forgiveness quickly picks us up again. Often we do not go in a straight line, but it does feel that we are going in the right direction. Our egos continue to do everything they can to make our task difficult.

The more space and acceptance I give to Diane and

others in my life, the more love I receive. The more I have let go of my old self-interests, and have the same interest in Diane and others as I do in myself, the more free and happy I have become.

I used to hold onto the many feelings that I would experience in a relationship. As I am learning to take more responsibility for my feelings, my need to hold on to "with-holds" diminishes.

When in conflict, Diane and I have found it helpful simply to ask for each other's help. The simple words *I need help* are magic, bringing about immediate listening with love. This response is quite different from before, when our egos wanted to attack or to defend themselves against what the other was saying, and we would end up choosing conflict rather than peace.

When either of us is upset, we ask the other if he or she feels safe enough to listen and to allow the other person to be insane for a few minutes and to perceive what we are about to say not as an attack but as a call for help and love. This helps us to avoid confrontations that end up in the old game of attack and defense, guilt, and judgments. It is amazing how unconditional love through listening can bring inner peace to us once again.

We find that starting and ending each day with remembering God and committing ourselves to peace of mind as our only goal is the best guarantee of having a peaceful day and a peaceful night.

The depth of unconditional love in our relationship has continued to grow as we have let go of our limitations. What is most important is that we are learning to let go of the arrogance of the ego writing its own script, or of our writing scripts for each other.

As our wills have become joined, our spiritual pathway has taken us to many places in the world. As co-directors of Children as Teachers of Peace, a project founded with friends in 1982, we have taken children to the People's Republic of China, the Soviet Union, and Central America. We feel privileged to have been catalysts for God to let the voices of children be heard around the world. It is our conviction that their hope and their clarity about peace is the hope for the world, and we feel blessed to travel with young children and to learn from them as much as we do.

We do our best each day to simplify our lives, to value and experience the preciousness of nature and of stillness. Rather than live as we did in the past, with five- and ten-year plans, we concentrate on living one day at a time, continuing to ask for guidance and direction each day.

At the time of this writing, our guidance is to put our energy into working with children and adults who have AIDS and to assist the health-care professionals who are working with them.

By awakening to my relationship with God through Diane and others, I have experienced and accepted unconditional love beyond what I ever imagined could be possible. I am becoming more consistent in knowing that there is no fight with God, and when I am in conflict, it is now easier for me to recognize that the fight and the fear that I experience are within my own mind.

I now know that relationships are only for joining and for experiencing the presence of God in one another. I am so grateful for the many gifts that God has given me through all the relationships I have had.

Many people are interested in the forms relationships take, so I am frequently asked what form I think my relationship with Diane will take in the future. I reply: "I don't know. What I do know is that we will always hold each other's hearts tenderly and gently. Regardless of whether our physical bodies are in the same place, our hearts will always be joined as one, with each other and with God, letting God's light shine through us to bring more light into a world that has been darkened by fear."

THE MIRACLE OF THE BUTTERFLY

Letting go and forgiveness are one and the same.
Their function is to let emotional attachment and
   investment in the past dissolve.

Their purpose is to let us experience
   Oneness with God.

When applied to "special relationships," letting go
   and forgiveness permit us to free ourselves
   from the imprisonment in someone else, under the
   guise that the other person has something we need.

Letting go and forgiveness are like
   transcending the barriers and limitations of the

cocoon, to become the essence of joy and freedom
and beauty that we see in the butterfly.

It is the Oneness we see when
    the color and hues of the butterfly's wings
    blend imperceptibly with a vibrant flower.

It allows us to experience the essence of our own love
    as One with everything in the Universe.

When we let go and forgive
    in a special relationship, we experience
    the miracle of immediately dissolving
    jealousy, possessiveness, exclusiveness,
    and the feelings of "missing."

The feeling of wanting to
    get something from another person;
    the need to control, manipulate, and
    predict the behavior of another person,
    simply vanishes.

The love/hate of special relationships,
    hating or loving according to whether
    one's imagined needs are met or not,
    also disappears.

The result of this miracle is that we remember and
    recognize that our only essence is Love,
    and Love needs nothing: its only function is to
    self-create.

The miracle of the butterfly is symbolically the
    transformation of a special relationship into

a Holy One, through letting go of the chains
of our self-imposed imprisonment.

The miracle of the butterfly is the knowledge that
we are One with each other and with God forever.

AIDS

TRANSFORMING FEAR INTO COMPASSION AND LOVE

Open your heart to God's Love
and any need you thought you had
will disappear.

The Challenge

AIDS has become the center of my focus. Without a doubt, this work is the greatest challenge of my life. In one sense, I feel that everything I have learned about attitudinal healing during these past years has been preparation for my work with people who have AIDS.

Never before have I experienced more tugging of my heart and testing of my beliefs than in working with young children and adults, in the prime of life, who have a disease that at this time has no cure.

My temptation to identify with the pain, suffering, and hopelessness these people experience has been great. I have also been tempted to renew my fight with God and to say that either there is an uncaring, cruel God or there is no God at all.

It is still difficult for me not to limit myself to a perceptual reality. To have peace of mind, I must remind myself, again and again, that I teach what I want to learn. And I am finding that attitudinal healing principles are extremely helpful for those who have AIDS, as well as for their friends and families.

Some of the underlying questions for me and the staff at the center have been:

1. How can we be helpful to people with AIDS and give them hope when their physicians say their disease is fatal?
2. How can we be helpful to the physicians and other health-care professionals who have felt the weight of helplessness, hopelessness, and depression? They see such a vast number of people die under their care, and because of this they may have their own fears about dying from AIDS.
3. How can we be helpful to the public at large, to the millions of people who are caught up in fear and hysteria and who lack adequate information?

The people who work at our center feel privileged to serve the individuals and families caught up in this crisis. We have witnessed courage beyond anything we had seen before. We have seen AIDS patients, their lovers, and their families express compassion, tenderness, gentleness, and unconditional love far beyond anything they had ever experienced before.

At times, we have seen AIDS victims rejected by their employers and co-workers, by their families, by some sectors of the medical and dental professions, and by some members of their home communities. We have witnessed people with AIDS demonstrating not anger, but total forgiveness—something I am not at all sure I could do if I were in their place. I am very fortunate to have been taught by these precious souls what true forgiveness, under the most difficult circumstances imaginable, is all about.

I have seen brave people who are very ill and frightened, as well as the people around them, honestly question their values and begin exploring some of life's most difficult questions: What is the purpose of life? What is true reality? Am I more than just this body? Is death the end of the line, or is life eternal? Is there a loving, creative force? Can I forgive the world for what I perceive is happening to me? Can I begin to live my life with the highest quality possible, one day at a time, giving unconditional love to all, living to give rather than to get? Can I live my life concerned about the content of love, rather than focused on the form of my body?

The Fear Epidemic

Perhaps nothing in modern times has caused more fear and hysteria than has AIDS. Today it is rapidly becoming a heterosexual disease, and it seems no person, age group, or country has a natural immunity.

What comes up for almost everyone is, "My God, this could happen to me!" The ego goes wild with the fear of our own deaths or the deaths of those close to us. Fear, preoccupation with death, and the thought that we might become innocent victims of the AIDS virus can begin to take over our minds. When this happens, the ego desperately seeks someone to blame.

We can become so blinded by our fear and anger that we may begin to attack others and separate from them. When we are fearful, we are prone to irrational behavior. For some people, the fear may become so consuming that, in blind desperation, they attack homosexuals, intravenous drug users, prostitutes, and even children who have AIDS and their parents.

The insane ego, in its effort to find someone to blame, will frequently point an accusing finger at God. When it rationalizes that God must be vengeful, we hear remarks such as "AIDS is God's way of punishing homosexuals for their sexual sins." The ego may go even further, implying that the parents of a child with AIDS are being punished for their misdeeds.

When fear builds a high wall around our minds and our hearts, it creates a state of darkness where it seems that neither forgiveness nor God can be found. We then develop distrust and paranoia and convince ourselves that these feelings are rational and intelligent.

When we are consumed by fear, anger, and hysteria, our minds refuse to take in new information, leaving us abandoned in a state of ignorance. Fear then produces a rigid state of mind that ignores the scientific evidence that AIDS can be transmitted only through sexual relations, sharing needles, or blood-to-blood interactions.

The fact that AIDS cannot be transmitted by casual contact—that it cannot be picked up in a restaurant, from a toilet seat, or from a sneeze, or from a place of business or a classroom—will be completely ignored by the fearful mind.

This fear, with its nearsighted perception, creates a world without love, compassion, and care, a world filled with separation. The ego then justifies that it is acceptable and rational to think of oneself first, even if this means hurting another person by firing him from a job, refusing to serve him in a restaurant, or barring a child from school.

Fear has led some people to seek legislation to quarantine people who have AIDS or who appear to be carrying the AIDS virus. This fear itself can become contagious. As the disease spreads globally, the fear of it spreads in tandem.

The AIDS crisis is no longer about Africa, Haiti, New York, and San Francisco. It is no longer a disease that affects "someone else." AIDS now affects every one of us. More than likely, in the near future no one will be exempt from having a family member, a friend, or an acquaintance who has this disease or is carrying the virus.

The AIDS crisis gives patients and all who come in contact with them an opportunity to examine closely what life is all about, what our purpose is, and what we feel about death. It gives us an opportunity to decide whether we want to concentrate on the quality and content of our lives or on the forms our lives take. And it provides us with a challenge to learn true compassion and unconditional love. In other words, it gives us a new opportunity for personal and spiritual transformation. It can be, for each of us, a time to recognize that our true identity is a spiritual one, not a physical one.

We can begin to discover another way of looking at healing, reminding ourselves that healing is letting go of the past and letting go of fear. We can then begin to consider that true healing may have less to do with the body and has *everything* to do with our hearts and our minds. It is time to heal fear and negative thoughts, not just bodies. It is time for us to let go of our fears of death and the future, and to believe that life and love are the same and that they are truly eternal.

William Blake once said: "When the doors of perception are cleansed, everything will appear to us as it is . . . infinite."

Our challenge today is to change the way we look at the world. We can then begin to experience a reality that transcends perception, a reality where there is no separation, where our only reality is love and God.

If there was ever a time not to turn our backs on love, it is now. With a caring attitude and with the same interest in every other soul as in ourselves, we can dismantle our self-built protective fences, open our hearts, and commit our trust and faith in love and a loving Creator.

This I believe is the challenge that each of us faces today: Are we willing to let love and compassion replace the fear that humankind has manufactured and become so attached to for so many centuries?

Has there ever been a better time than this very second to make the decision to value only love, not fear?

The AIDS Programs at the Center for Attitudinal Healing

I became actively interested in the AIDS issue in 1982. I thought that our Center for Attitudinal Healing had some valid tools to offer the public as well as those with AIDS. I did not realize then that it would be a new opportunity for me to test my faith in God.

I have been most blessed by having as my teachers children with AIDS and their parents, adults with AIDS and their lovers, friends and families of people with AIDS, and the many co-workers who have worked at our center.

In 1983 I talked to the center's director, the staff, and the board of directors about extending our work to include AIDS patients and their families. Although many staff members were open to the idea, others stated that they were too overworked to extend themselves further. I also encountered resistance from some of the center's patients.

The staff members who were in favor of working with AIDS wondered if fear, not just overwork, was holding the others back. Since the center is based on choosing love rather than fear, we felt that we needed to heal our own fears before we could go on.

Clearly, an intense educational approach was necessary for our center. We had experts on AIDS speak to our staff, and we also visited AIDS treatment centers. It took about six months before the staff let go of fear and decided to help in this crisis. And I learned another important lesson about not making assumptions.

There was a staff decision to integrate the AIDS patients with the people who had other catastrophic illnesses. As always, there was to be no charge for our services. Groups met on Tuesday mornings and Tuesday evenings, and on Tuesday evenings there was also a support group for family members, friends, and lovers. This worked out amazingly well.

About six months after the program started, the

AIDS patients asked if we would start an additional group, exclusively for them. They still saw value in the general groups, but they wanted a group that dealt only with AIDS.

Today, about half of our AIDS patients go to both groups. Our staff also spends a great deal of time making home visits and going to hospitals. Recently we started a "Well but Worried" group for those who have been tested as "HIV sero positive," which means they've been infected with the AIDS virus but have no active disease.

We are seeing children with AIDS and their families, and children who are HIV sero positive. We have traveled throughout the country visiting such children.

We have also been working with Hemophiliac Societies and with hemophiliacs who are HIV sero positive. In addition, we have also started a national "AIDS Hotline for Kids," which is both a support group and an information network. Our friend Jack Keeler, a cartoonist, has created a poster that is being used nationally and internationally to help spread the word about the work at our and similar centers. It is a drawing of a small child with a sad expression; at the bottom of the poster it says: I HAVE AIDS. PLEASE HUG ME. I CAN'T MAKE YOU SICK. It has appeared in numerous magazines, including *Newsweek*, on billboards, and on television, in several different countries.

(To obtain a copy of the poster, write: Center for Attitudinal Healing, AIDS Hotline for Kids, 19 Main Street, Tiburon, CA 94920, or call 415-435-5022. Please send $2.00 for postage and handling.)

I HAVE AIDS
PLease hug me

I can't make you sick

J. Keeler c.1987

AIDS HOT LINE FOR KIDS
CENTER FOR ATTITUDINAL HEALING
19 MAIN ST., TIBURON, CA 94920, (415) 435-5022

I would like to share with you some stories about the brave people I have worked with and who have been my teachers. Their stories demonstrate the practical applications of attitudinal healing principles.

The first AIDS patient I saw was a young man named William Calderon. He was a hairdresser and was co-owner with his lover, Henry, of a well-established salon. One of William's clients, Judith Skutch Whitson, had been a beacon of light and support for him. She continued to tell him that nothing was impossible and that he should never give up hope.

Judy demonstrated her lack of fear by hugging and kissing him every time she had a hair appointment. She had given him a copy of *Love Is Letting Go of Fear* and had introduced him to the writing of Dr. Carl Simonton. There had been magazine articles about William as the person who had lived with AIDS the longest and who was still in good health. It was Judy who introduced me to William.

William, Henry, and I became involved in fundraising efforts for an AIDS foundation in Los Angeles. William and Henry provided a special model of unconditional love. Henry did not desert his partner when they discovered he had AIDS. Although they took all the precautions advised by medical authorities, Henry was not afraid of AIDS.

Together they taught each other, and many others, including me, much about gentleness and patience. The three of us became very close friends. Henry and William began to reevaluate the quality of their lives as well as their life-style, and they began to spend much of their time helping others.

Their greatest joy came from their work in assisting others who were immobilized with fear and terror. When a person puts all his attention and energy into helping other people, he begins to lose his awareness and preoccupation with his own body.

This is what happened to William, and the process began opening doors to experiencing the peace of God. William's initial fight with God began to dissipate. I learned a lot about my own fight with God by working with William.

After having the disease for about six years, William's condition worsened. He and I had always hugged and kissed each other on the cheek when we met. One day when I visited William at his home, I noticed lesions over a large area of his body. As I hugged him and went to kiss him on the cheek, I heard a voice in my mind that I did not want to believe.

I was certain that I had no fear of AIDS, yet there was the voice of my ego, saying, "You'd better be careful; are you sure you want to kiss his cheek?" I was ashamed and felt like a hypocrite. But then I remembered the story about St. Francis of Assisi. His life was changed when he hugged a person with leprosy, after initially hesitating. He overcame his fear and saw only the light of love in that person, rather than identifying with the body and the deadly disease affecting it.

I quickly gave my friend the usual hug and kiss on the cheek.

In the flash of that second I saw only the essence and

light of love in William, and I felt a light joining us as one. Love had replaced fear. William then went on to share with me, more deeply than he had before, some of his own fears about dying.

William worked as hard at healing his relationships as anyone I know. There were old unhealed relationships with family members, and there were newer relationships that challenged him—clients, doctors, advisers, and so on. More and more William became a beacon of light. It was rare that I did not see that wonderful, warm smile on his face.

William was very clear about his funeral. He wanted it to be a celebration of life. He wanted happy music, which he picked himself, he wanted the ceremony to be at his and Henry's home, and he wanted me to conduct the memorial service. One of William's and my favorite prayers was the Prayer of St. Francis of Assisi.

During William's last weeks I saw him almost daily at his home. He liked me to recite that prayer, and when I did, I could see the light go on in his eyes, even when he was no longer able to talk. William came to know that his mission was to light up everyone who came to visit him, knowing that often they were fearful and didn't know what to say.

He saw that his purpose was to share with all who came to see him his faith and trust in the peace of God. I saw him undergo a spiritual transformation. Everyone who knew William saw him as one of the strongest teachers of courage, patience, faith, and trust they had ever known.

All of us who were privileged to know William during his short stay here, and who saw him as our teacher, continue to experience the presence of his love within us.

Children with AIDS

Diane and I flew to Indiana to see Ryan White not long after he was diagnosed as having AIDS. Ryan had been infected with the virus through a blood transfusion. When we first saw him he was quite ill, and no one knew whether he would live or die. During that visit, Jeanie, his mother, told us the history of Ryan's illness and how it had affected her, her daughter, and Ryan. Jeanie also told us of the amazing transformation that had taken place, where hate and anger had been transformed into love.

Jeanie told us that when Ryan came down with AIDS, even though she had never met a homosexual, she began to hate them as a group. She immediately lost her faith in God. A short time later, she was in New York City telling her story on national television. While there, she was asked to visit the AIDS ward at Bellevue Hospital.

During that visit, Jeanie's perception began to change. There on the ward, she suddenly saw homosexuals not as evil, sexual monsters, but as human beings who were very frightened and who were asking for love.

Two days later, another remarkable event took place. Jeanie received a telephone call from a woman in the Midwest who had seen her on television. The woman said that she had just received a call from her twenty-five-year-old son, who had told her two things that she had not known previously: First, he told her that he was a homosexual, and second, he told her that he had had AIDS for over three years. He wanted to come home to die. With much anguish in her voice, the mother asked Jeanie what to do.

Without a moment's hesitation, Jeanie replied, "The biggest gift that you can give yourself, the most beautiful gift you can give your son, and the greatest gift of love you can give to God is to ask your son to come home. Love him, care for him, give all your worries to God, and do not fear." The mother did just that.

Jeanie and the woman became friends, and Ryan frequently got on the phone with the woman's son, to cheer him up and to give him hope, and to share his feelings about having AIDS.

Diane and I were deeply impressed and humbled by the way Jeanie had changed her perceptions of the world. She had crossed the bridge of forgiveness and had begun to experience peace and love and God returning to her heart. It was clear to us both that we were not there to help so much as to learn from the Whites. Diane and I were blessed to have such wonderful teachers in our lives.

When Ryan became better and his physicians said he could return to school—that he was no longer a danger to others—his school refused to admit him. Once again there was a great temptation for Jeanie to be angry and to feel victimized. It took a lawyer and much legal maneuvering to get the school's decision reversed.

One day, while watching the local television news,

Jeanie saw a group of angry parents saying they were going to boycott Ryan's school. Suddenly a little girl, about Ryan's age, popped up among the parents and said, "I'm not afraid of getting AIDS. And there are lots of kids like me here. Ryan needs love and friendship and we want to give him both."

Suddenly Jeanie felt God's presence, and once again forgiveness, hope, and peace returned to her heart. Rather than seeing attacking parents, she began to perceive them as fearful.

Later the Whites moved to another community, which has been accepting, loving, caring, and helpful. Ryan and his family continue to help others. Many times I have phoned them to put them in touch with others on our AIDS Hotline for Kids, and they have never once refused. They know that giving and receiving are the same. I am delighted that the world will now hear their courageous story, for preparations are under way for a television movie about Ryan White and his family.

Over and over again we are given opportunities to consider the possibility that everything that happens to us gives us a new chance to choose what we believe and what we see in our lives. It is possible to transcend even the worst tragedy and despair that the ego would have us perceive. We can choose to see only life, light, and love.

Angels of Mercy

At our center we have seen foster parents choose to bring children with AIDS into their homes. Many of these children are infants who were born with the disease. Frequently, the natural mothers were intravenous drug users and were unable to care for their children. Unfortunately, these children are often rejected by their communities, families, and friends.

I call the foster parents of these children Angels of Mercy. Some of them, too, have been subjected to rejection by their friends and neighbors.

I recently talked to a foster mother whose AIDS infant had died just a week before. She was not afraid of contracting AIDS, and she wanted to take care of another AIDS baby as soon as possible. These foster mothers are teaching me and all who know them the power of unconditional love and what serving is all about.

They are truly messengers of God.

For me one of the most remarkable teachers for helping me to stop my fight with God has been Ava Jean and her family. Following the death of her husband from cancer, she found out that her two sons were gay. Later, her older son came down with AIDS, and she, her son, and her son's lover began coming to the center. Her son later died but Ava Jean was able to find a quiet peace in God.

Ava Jean and her son's lover continued to attend the center. There, it was confirmed for her that when physical healing is not possible, spiritual healing can occur. That fact can change the lives of people with AIDS.

Later Peter, Ava Jean's youngest son, developed AIDS and died.

I had dinner with Peter a few months before his death and he told me that in the last year there had been a tremendous change in the quality of his life. He said it was akin to feeling, on the highest level, the experience of oneness with God, an experience that for him goes beyond any kind of theology. He said he is learning that *living in the consciousness of giving* is what life is about. Everyone who knew Peter saw his light shining brighter than the sun. Peter died at his home in the middle of July 1988.

With the kind of history A.J. has had, one might think that she would be bitter, angry at the world and at God, and having a difficult time with life. The situation is quite the opposite. A.J. has learned to depend on God. She is involved with her local Episcopal church and volunteers at a hospital as a lay chaplain. She frequently sees parents from parts of the country where AIDS and homosexuality are still issues of shame. The isolation from human contact adds to these parents' misery. For them, talking to A.J. is enormously helpful and inspiring.

❦

Diane, the center's staff, and I have been privileged to work with hospitals and public agencies involved in the AIDS crisis. In most of these organizations, everyone is overworked, and there is little time to process one's own feelings. In addition, most health-care workers were trained to hide their real feelings in their professional lives.

Seeing so many people die—people who have become your friends—is frequently the number-one source of stress for health-care professionals. But many of these workers are beginning to recognize that death doesn't have to be seen as a failure.

We recently put on a conference with San Francisco General Hospital on meeting the emotional and psychological needs of professionals and support people working with AIDS. We have found that group interactions, based on the principles of attitudinal healing, have been most helpful for many of these professionals. And we have been encouraged to extend this work.

Spiritual Transformation and Crisis

The commitment of the health-care workers and the ability of the patients, their lovers, and their families to turn pain and fear into compassion and unconditional love are all deeply moving experiences. When we see that our purpose in life is to join together, to help and love one another, we can begin to experience our true spiritual nature. When you are dedicated to giving, loving, and helping others, there is no longer any fight with God.

I believe with all my heart that as more and more of us begin to experience love and forgiveness as our only functions, we will begin to see that unconditional love is the answer to all our problems and to all our questions.

I feel that through the tragedy of AIDS there is an awakening for many of us: a realization that we are spirit, not ego; that there is only life, not death; that there is no separation, there is only love.

BEYOND SUFFERING

Remind me that when I am in
    the Heart of God, there is
    no suffering. There is no pain.

Help me to be compassionate and
    identify with the dignity of Love
    in all whom my eyes would behold.

Remind me that the gift
    of peace and unconditional love
    is the most valuable thing
    I can give to anyone.

Let me look past the pain that
    human suffering would tempt me
    to identify with
    and to see only the Light of Love
    enveloping and emanating from
    all living forms.

Help me to know that Your Love
    is my only reality
    and to know that what is true and real
    can never be hurt or harmed.

Let me be the beacon of Your Light
    that heals all pain, suffering,
    and separation.

Let me feel the beating of Your Heart
    within me, that I may shine
    Your Love and Light on all
    and know that the Light I see
    is but a reflection of Your Light
    and my Light joined as One.

Remind me to be grateful for Your Love
    and for the opportunity to be
    helpful and loving to all others.

CHAPTER

16

EVERYONE
IS OUR
TEACHER

EACH OF US CAN MAKE A DIFFERENCE

Each of us can make a difference
  When we put an end to *in*difference and
  When we let go of our selfish desires.

Each of us makes a difference
  When we awaken each day
  By showing each other the way.

Each of us makes a difference
  When we commit ourselves to have a heart
  That beats only with compassion,
  Where caring for one another becomes
  Our only passion.

Each of us makes a difference
  When giving, kindness, patience, and tenderness
  Is the way that we pray,
  When Love and Forgiveness become
  Our song of the day.

Each of us can make a difference
  When everything we think, say, or do
  Becomes a gift of Love to God.

Each of us makes a difference
  When we commit ourselves
  To Peace, to Love, to Happiness;
  When we commit our lives to God.

When we choose to remember that everyone we meet along the path of life is our teacher of forgiveness, of love, and of the presence of God, life begins to have new meaning and purpose. The ego, however, would have us see people as teachers of fear. When we let go of our judgments and put the ego aside, chaos, despair, depression, and conflict begin to disappear, replaced by love and happiness.

I am constantly reminded that there are no accidental meetings in life, and when we see that we are all equals—as teacher/student and student/teacher—every relationship can come to light as a new opportunity to experience the presence of love, and of God in each other.

I would like to share with you some of the stories of people who have been my teachers.

While in Denver to give a speech, I stopped to get my shoes shined. I was with a friend, and as she and I were talking, I noticed the enthusiasm with which the man was shining my shoes. My shoes had never had more tender loving care. The man was smiling from ear to ear; he seemed in a state of bliss. It took him more than fifteen minutes to shine my shoes. When I told him that no one had ever taken such care with my shoes before, he replied that it was his "gift to God."

When I asked him to explain, he said he felt blessed in being a child of God and in receiving God's abundant love. Because of his appreciation for God's love, he makes certain that whatever he does is done as a gift to God.

He told me he felt God's presence in everything he sees or touches. As he spoke, it became clear that in shining my shoes so lovingly, he was expressing his love for God. Watching him was almost like watching a person in a blissful state of meditation or prayer.

I found both tremendous humility and profound happiness in this man. He taught me that everything we do in life can be a gift to God. He reminded me that with every "hello," with everyone we touch, with everything we do, even if it is cleaning toilets, it can be done with all of our love as a gift to God.

In a most unexpected way, having my shoes shined that day proved to be a powerful spiritual experience. The man exemplified that it is not *what* we do but *how* we do it that matters.

That night, I focused my lecture on finding the presence of God in everything we do—including getting your shoes shined.

❦

During a break in a lecture one day, a little boy, about five years old, came up to me and asked with great wonder, "Hey, mister, what were you like when you were new?" What a powerful and deep question that was!

I was most grateful that he had asked, and I appreciated the originality of the question. Children are like a breath of fresh air as they express how they see the world. We have much to learn from them.

In answer to the little boy I said that when I was *new,* "I was full of love and innocence, just like you." But the truth is that I continued to ponder the boy's question for days. With thanks to this child, I began to wonder when I, like so many others, lost that feeling of being full of love and innocence. I reminded myself that the newborn infant is the essence of innocence, full of love, light, faith, trust, and happiness.

Love and innocence fly out the window the moment we begin judging others or ourselves. And we recapture that innocence the moment we stop making judgments. In my daily meditations I pictured that little boy. I let his image remind me that every day can be a newly experienced birth, where I once again view everything with the newness of a child.

Bobby came to our center and taught me much about dealing with anger. He was ten years old and his kidneys were seriously diseased. He was waiting for a transplant.

Both of Bobby's parents had been born deaf and mute, so sign language was the first language Bobby learned. Verbal speech was his second language.

Whenever he and his parents went to the doctor's office, Bobby would tell his parents, through sign language, what the physician said.

One day I began to wonder about growing up in Bobby's family. I tried to imagine what it was like when Bobby's father was angry at him. Finally, I asked, "What do you do when your dad is using sign language to tell you he's angry at you?"

Bobby's eyes twinkled and he grinned. "Oh, I just close my eyes," he said.

❦

I will never forget Greg Harrison, the first child from our center who died. He died at eleven years of age. In August 1987, ten years after his death, I had lunch with his parents. We discussed how Greg, like so many of the children we see at the center, was a wise soul in a young body, one who had come to teach the truth to those who would listen.

Greg's medical history was typical of many children we see at the center. After having been on almost a dozen drugs, all of which had terrible side effects, Greg took part in a decision to discontinue medication.

Greg's pediatrician told him that without medication he probably would die within a few weeks. During the next group meeting at the center, one of the other kids asked Greg, "What's it like to know you might be dead in a few weeks?" Greg replied with great peace and tranquility, "I think when you die you simply lay aside your body, which was never real in the first place. And then you are at one with all other souls and God." He added, "Sometimes, you come back as someone's guardian angel."

Greg gave us all another way of looking at life and death. He did not think, for even one moment, that death was the end of the line.

I am very grateful to Greg and the many other children I've met, all of whom have helped me see another way of viewing the world, and who have given me the courage to trust. There has never been a doubt in my mind that Greg continues to serve as my guardian angel, helping me through the rough spots that I have manufactured for myself.

The Eternal Dance of Light and Life

A few years ago I had a wonderful dream. I was on a mountaintop. There was a large circle of children around me, all of whom I had worked with before they died. In my dream we were all holding hands, joyfully dancing in a circle. Then we were joined by the adults I have worked with. It did not feel like a dream; it felt very real.

It was so beautiful that I began crying with joy. Then they put me in the center of their circle, and as they danced around me they floated up into the air, making a spiral as they ascended.

Then a most remarkable thing happened. As each person rose higher, they blew me kisses, and in that instant their bodies were transformed into light. It was spectacular.

In experiencing the dream, I believed that my

friends, my teachers from the other side, were telling me that life is a dance of light and happiness, and there is no death.

❦

Sharon Winter came to our center when she was a teenager. She had cancer. I remember how cautious and guarded she was the first time she attended a meeting. She did not think she had much in common with the other children, who were all much younger than she.

Sharon soon changed her mind. She worked hard at applying attitudinal healing principles in her life. It wasn't easy. She felt that she had spent the first year of her illness being misdiagnosed, and she believed things would have been much better for her if the doctors had correctly diagnosed her sooner. Quite understandably, forgiveness didn't come easily to her.

She was an extremely attractive girl, and losing her hair in chemotherapy was most difficult for her. But the cancer disappeared, and after a number of years she married. It looked as if things were going well for her. Then the cancer returned.

By this time Sharon and her family had become my extended family. She and her husband often stayed in my home when I was out of town.

Sharon taught me much about courage, trust, honoring the self, and the many ways in which the mind can control the body. For example, when my son Lee received his Ph.D., Sharon was invited to a party celebrating the event. Her cancer had progressed, and when I visited her at the hospital the day of the party, she was on intravenous morphine and looked close to death. However, she was certain that she would be at the party. Looking at her, I could not imagine how she could possibly make it.

Sharon did show up at the party. No one would have known that she was ill. I couldn't believe my eyes—she was vivacious and looked angelic. As far as I was concerned, she was a walking miracle.

Sharon didn't allow her physical condition to stop her that night. I believe that she created such a strong mental picture of attending the party and enjoying herself that she literally created her own reality, one that allowed her to transcend her physical condition.

When I visited her the next day at the hospital, Sharon looked pale and gray again, but she was very pleased with herself. After my visit, Sharon left the hospital and went home, where a short time later she died.

I never had an opportunity to meet him in person, but the story of Manuel Garcia, his family, and his friends will always have a special place in my heart, for it taught me that even in the most tragic of circumstances, love can replace fear, and happiness and joy can be found; that even in our darkest moments, God's love can light the path. The Garcia family demonstrated, in the most graphic terms imaginable, the true meaning of the phrase *out of darkness into the light*.

When he was thirty-nine, Manuel discovered that he had cancer. Through chemotherapy he lost all his hair and more than sixty pounds. The doctors were concerned. Seeing his body failing, he had trouble keeping up hope. A part of him felt abandoned by God. His plan for his life was obviously not working out, and he was afraid of what would happen to his family if he died.

On the day he was to be discharged from the hospital, he felt tired and apprehensive. While waiting for his wife and friends to come to his room to pick him up, he fell asleep. He was not sure if he was dreaming when suddenly he felt the footsteps of people shuffling around his bed. He opened his eyes and was astonished. Over the bedrail he saw five completely shaved heads. Looking more closely, he realized it wasn't a dream. The bald heads belonged to his wife and four friends.

He blinked and shook his head to make certain he was awake. Then everyone burst out laughing. Their laughter echoed through the halls of the hospital, uplifting everyone's spirits.

They drove home, and as Manuel opened the door he was met by more than fifty relatives and friends, children and adults of all ages. Every one of them had a shaved head.

There was a celebration of love that day that no one will ever forget. In that moment, Manuel's feelings of separation vanished. There was no fear. There was only love.

Later, during the party, Manuel shared his thanks with everyone, and he thanked God for reminding him that God's love is always present. That day, all his thoughts of being abandoned by God vanished, and I am certain that everyone there experienced giving and receiving as the same.

David Roth wrote a song about Manuel and his friends, entitled, appropriately, "Manuel Garcia." The lyrics are as follows:

Manuel Garcia, a proud youthful father
Was known on his block as a hardworking man
With a wife and a family, a job with a future.
He'd everything going according to plan . . .

One day Manuel Garcia, complaining of stomach
    pains
Went to the clinic to find out the cause.
His body was found to have cancerous tissue
Ignoring the order of natural laws . . .

So Manuel Garcia of Milwaukee County
Checked into the medical complex in town
Suddenly seeing his thirty-nine years
Like the sand in an hourglass plummeting down . . .

"What are my choices?" cried Manuel Garcia.
"You've basically two," was the doctor's decree.
"Your cancer untreated will quickly be fatal,
But treatment is painful, with no guarantees . . ."

And so it began, Manuel's personal odyssey,
Long, sleepless nights in a chemical daze
With echoes of footsteps down long, lonely corridors
Tolling the minutes and hours away . . .

With the knowlege that something inside was
    consuming him,

Manuel Garcia was filled with despair.
He'd already lost forty pounds to the cancer
And now to the drugs he was losing his hair . . .

After nine weeks in treatment his doctor came calling,
Said, "Manuel, we've done all we can do.
Your cancer can go either way at this juncture.
It is out of our hands, and it's now up to you . . ."

He looked into the mirror, a sad, frightened stranger
So pale, so wrinkled, so lonely, scared,
Diseased, isolated, and feeling unlovable,
One hundred twenty-six pounds and no hair . . .

He dreamed of his Carmen at sixty without him,
His four little children not having a dad,
Of Thursday night card games at Julio's, and
     everything else.
He'd not done what he wished that he had . . .

Awakened from sleep on the day of his discharge
By shuffling feet going all round his bed,
Manuel opened his eyes and thought he was still
     dreaming.
His wife and four friends with no hair on their heads . . .

He blinked and he looked again, not quite believing
The four shiney heads all lined up side by side.
And still to this point not a word had been spoken
But soon they were laughing so hard that they cried . . .

The hospital hallways were ringing with voices,
"Patron, we did this for you," said his friends.
And they wheeled him out to the car they had
     borrowed.
     "Amigo, estamos, contigo, ves . . ."

So Manuel Garcia returned to his neighborhood,
Dropped off in front of his two-bedroom flat.
The block seemed unusually deserted for Sunday.
He took a deep breath and adjusted his hat . . .

But before he could enter, the front door flew
    open.
Manuel was surrounded with faces he knew.
Fifty-odd loved ones and friends of the family
With clean-shaven heads and the words "We love you . . ."

And so Manuel Garcia, a victim of cancer,
A father, a husband, a neighbor and friend
With a lump in his throat said, "I'm not one for
    speeches
But here I have something that needs to be said . . .

"I felt all alone with my baldness and cancer.
Now you stand beside me, thank Heaven above
For giving me strength that I need, may God
    bless you
And long may we live with the meaning of love . . .

"For giving me strength that I need, may God
    bless you
And long may we live with the meaning of love . . ."

God Is in Every Relationship

As I continue to learn from the people I meet and work
with, my spiritual path becomes a little easier and a little clearer. Each new lesson reminds me to let go of
judgments and concentrate on seeing the light of love,
the God-self, in others. And I have begun to see that
everyone who has ever touched my life has provided

one more lesson for me in the true meaning of forgiveness and unconditional love. I am grateful to all of them, for they have taught me to see the world differently.

Each day I am tempted to go back to my old judgmental ways. Each day I must remind myself that human perception is a mirror, not a fact. And each day it becomes a little easier to see the holiness in all of us.

CHAPTER

17

NOTHING IS
IMPOSSIBLE

When you have faith and trust in God,
nothing is impossible;
there is always hope,
there is always joy,
there is always love,
and there is always
tranquility and peace.

While writing this book, I told a friend that there were times when I found it difficult to write. I had to laugh when he suggested that maybe I was still fighting with God.

I admit that I am still tempted to fight. Of course, in my saner moments I know that God was never engaged in the fight and never will be, and that the only opponent is within my own conflicted mind.

We can learn much by looking at the contrasts between different times in our lives. And the contrasts for me between 1975 and now reveal how much my relationship with God has changed.

In 1975 I would have judged anyone out of his mind who even suggested that I would turn my life over to God, that I would stop drinking, that I would found the Center for Attitudinal Healing, that I would become an author, and that so many people would come into my life to teach me forgiveness and love. I would not have believed that I could learn to accept and love myself— and to love others as well. My ego would have said that all these things were impossible. And if anyone had told me that I would have intimate relationships based love, not fear, I would have said that this, too, was impossible.

Today, guided by a very different belief system, I believe that nothing is impossible. As my trust and faith in God deepens, I see that love is the only reality there is.

Before these changes in my life, I clung to guilt with all my might. Today, that old attraction to guilt is fading; I no longer believe that it is an inescapable, hereditary condition.

I once believed that everyone was to blame. Now I believe there simply is no blame.

Previously, I believed that peace of mind was impossible. Now there are times when I experience peace of mind beyond my fondest imaginings.

Before 1975, I thought that I could not be peaceful unless other people in my life changed. Today, when I am irritated, angry, or depressed, I can *choose* to change my thoughts and experience peace of mind.

Previously, I thought that the purpose of *time* was for me to perform and to judge my performance, and this meant that I faced an endless series of tests and inevitable failures. Now I see time as offering infinite opportunities to choose once again, presenting new possibilities to change my mind.

Once I was compulsively interested in the *forms* of the world. Now I am increasingly centered on the *content* of life—that is, on love.

Before, I felt that mistakes were not acceptable; if I made one, I felt I had committed an unpardonable sin.

Today, I see that we learn from mistakes and that errors can be corrected. Less and less do I stick myself with guilt.

❦

Sometimes we have unhealed relationships even before we first encounter someone or something. I had an unhealed relationship with computers before I ever worked with one. Writing this book has produced another miracle for me, one centered in the practicalities of life. In 1975 my greatest fear was that of dying. In 1987 if someone had asked me the same question I would have answered that it was my fear of computers.

Because of my dyslexia, I had convinced myself that I could never learn to use a computer. I reasoned that I was more comfortable writing by hand, then cutting and pasting my notes together. I had decided *never even to try* working with a computer. There was my ego again, telling me of another potential failure.

My guidance, however, told me that I was to learn how to use a computer and to write this book on one. Then an old friend, Chet Watson, offered to help. If ever there was a teacher of patience, love, and gentleness, it is Chet. To my amazement and delight, he taught me to use a word processor, one step at a time. I am very grateful to Chet, for his patience, love, and support were exactly what I needed.

I wrote this entire book on my computer. By listening to my inner voice, I was able to lay aside yet another one of my self-imposed limitations, and once again I was reminded that nothing is impossible.

In the next chapter I'll discuss ways of stilling the mind through prayers and meditation. As I was preparing to write that chapter, I remembered an old saying from India:

> A busy mind is a sick mind;
> A slow mind is a healthy mind;
> And a still mind is a divine mind.

The more we can remove ourselves from the busyness of the world, the better we can still our minds, and the more we will feel the presence and hear the voice of God.

CHAPTER

18

MEDITATIONS FOR DAILY USE

Prayer is the food of the soul.

When I go to bed, I frequently ask my inner teacher for help. Sometimes I ask for assistance with a specific problem; at other times I ask for help with letting go of my ego and surrendering to God.

Often I awaken in the middle of the night with the urge to write. Sometimes I write a few sentences, and sometimes I write a page or so in the form of a meditation.

I have selected from these writings the ones that I have found most helpful as morning meditations. I hope that you, too, will find them helpful.

For me, meditations are for stilling the mind, for experiencing the peace and love of God, for removing the blocks to the awareness of love's presence, and for opening the heart and mind to God's direction.

ON MEDITATION

What is meditation but an effort
   to experience God's Love.
It is getting away from the
   multitudinous thoughts and tensions
   of the unfinished business
   of our external life;
It is a willingness
   simply to be still
And to listen.

I wrote the following after returning from a visit to refugee camps in Sudan in March 1985, a time when there was much starvation and many deaths. I learned a great deal about commitment from the many volunteers whom it was my good fortune to meet.

COMMITMENT

To be peaceful and joyful, there is but
   one commitment to make.

It is to live life, one second at a time,
   as if it is an eternal moment.
It is to make the decision,
   regardless of the behavior we observe,
   no matter where we are,
   nor whom we are with,

To be a vehicle of God's Perfect Love,
To be totally accepting and defenseless,
To give all of ourselves away in Love,
To give total, maximal, and unconditional Love
      to everyone, excluding no one.

It is to make the commitment
   with every thought,
   with every breath,
   with every heartbeat,

To be helpful to those in need,
   who are crying out for help and
   are suffering because of lack of love.

It is to make the decision
   to have the fire of compassion in our hearts,
   to love the universe and all that is in it
      with tender loving care.

It is to make the decision to trust and
   accept God's boundless Love for ourselves,
   and thereby, become a messenger of God's Love.
It is to demonstrate and teach only Love,
   for that is what we are.

HONESTY

To be honest is to demonstrate
   a total lack of any deception.
It is to omit nothing
   because of our own fears
   of being attacked or rejected.

To be honest we must be
   totally free of guilt and fear,
   to recognize that either
   we are honest—or we are not;
   and there is no in-between.

To be honest is to experience the
   perfect harmony of having only
   loving thoughts, loving words,
   and loving deeds.

It is to take full responsibility
   for our own behavior and
   to blame no one for anything.

To be honest is to be perfectly free
   and unafraid to be exactly
   what we are . . . LOVE.

LET US TAKE EACH OTHER'S HANDS

Let us take each other's hands
  and walk toward the light of God.
Let us stay in the presence of God
  and in the nowness of Joy.

Let us be free from separation
  of all kinds.
Let us resist the temptation
  to judge each other's behavior.

Let us stop our suffering.
Let us, together, once and for all,
  let go of all our past hurts,
  and unmet desires.
Let us put our total trust in God and
  then see only the God-Self in each other
  and feel God's never-ending Love
  filling us to the brim and over.

Let us let go of all our self-doubts
  that we have projected to each other.
Let us join our wills as one
  and be directed only by God's Plan.

Let us join in Love
Let us join in Joy
Let us join in Peace.
Let us LOVE, LOVE, LOVE . . .

THE ANSWER

Many problems seem impossible
  because we concentrate on the problem
  rather than the answer.

Love is the only answer,
  and when we focus only on Love,
  all of our problems will disappear.

FORGIVE

Forgive,
Forgive,
And forgive some more;

Never stop forgiving,
For the temptation to project
  and judge will always be there
  as long as you are living in the body.

Forgiveness is the key to peace and happiness,
    and gives us everything
    that we could possibly want.

PATIENCE

The impatient are always
  in a hurry.
They are trapped in the future
  attached to fear and time.
The impatient follow self-made
  goals that go nowhere.

The patient are never
  in a hurry.
They are totally in the present,
  bathed in timeless loving.
The patient have no need for goals,
  except to be Home
  in the Heart of God.

The patient are patient
  because they know
  they are already there.

LOVING

May your loving
  be like your breathing,
Smooth and easy,
  free flowing,
  effortless,
  continual,
  with no interruptions,
Breathing in God's limitless Love
And breathing out
  the boundless love
  that is in your heart.

I AM

I am the Will of God.

I am the purity of love, joy, and peace united as one.
I am the essence of giving and of joining.
I am the state of mind
   where there is total absence of fear, guilt,
   anger and hate,
   pain and sickness,
   and of judgment and separation of any kind.
I am the reflection of God's Love,
   and hence, I am everywhere;
   I have no boundaries and no form.

I am the light of the world,
   and hence, I am a reflection of all that is beautiful.
I am a reflection of the simplicity of
   the flowers, the sand on the beach,
   the singing of the birds,
   the sound of the waves on the shore,
   and the stillness of the lake.
I am a reflection of all that
   is gentle, kind, tender, compassionate, and
   of all that is trusting and honest.
I am that state of mind
   where there is only eternal life,
   and there is no death; and
   where there is only happiness.

I am the essence of Spirit,
   and it is my spiritual being that is my identity.
I am whole and united with all life.
I am invisible and immeasurable.
I am God's Holy Child of Love;
I am God's Creation; God is my Cause, and
   I am God's Effect.
I am co-creator of Love with God.

God's Will and my will are one.
If ever I accept anything else as my will,
I deny what I am.

I am a reflection of the Will of God.

SPECK OF FEAR

As it takes only one speck of dirt
   to destroy the purity of clear water
It takes but one speck of fear
   to hide the presence of Love.

Bliss is that state of being
   when we are bathed
      in our gratefulness for the
         boundless serenity of love of
            our Creator—and
               at the same time,
                  we are accepting God's
                  gratitude to us.

CHAPTER
19

EVERY STEP
OF THE WAY

Recently I saw the following poem from a twelve-year-old girl who wrote her thoughts about peace for a book I helped put together, Children as Teachers of Peace, published in 1982.

I was reminded of the importance of clarity and simplicity. This young girl said in one sentence what I have taken a whole book trying to say.

Her statement is so important to me that I have devoted this entire chapter to it.

When I grow up, I hope I can be like her. At the times when I am able to take her statement to heart, I have only perfect trust, and I have no fight with God.

I believe that if each of us would make her teaching a prayer for every moment of our lives, the universe would be filled only with peace and love.

"Peace is when
You know that God
Is holding your hand
Every step of the way."

CHAPTER

20

"LOVE
IS THE WAY I WALK
IN GRATITUDE"

IN GRATITUDE TO YOU

My whole being pulsates
   with the fire of desire
   for our everlasting union.
My very breath is but Yours.
My heart is a limitless beacon
   of Your Love.

My Spirit, being Yours, is the light of the world.
My eyes but radiate and reflect
   our Perfect Love.
My very essence vibrates with You as the
   harmony of music not yet heard.

My vision is but Your Love
   flowing through me,
   seeing only its own reflection.
My only fulfillment is following Your
   Directions and Guidance.

My voice, being Yours, can only bless.
My prayer is but an eternal song of gratitude,
That You are in me, and I am in You,
And that I live in Your Grace forever.

Can there be anything more important than acknowledging others by saying just these two words: "Thank you."

When we are stuck in our minds and we believe that the world we perceive is all that there is, the ego feels justified in complaining about all the catastrophes around us. "Thank you" is not a phrase the ego finds easy to say. The ego wants to cling to the belief that we are victims of people and circumstances outside ourselves.

The ego would have us believe that love and peace are not possible in this world. Rather than having us thank one another, it would have us attack one another.

If it could, the ego would forever hide from our awareness the fact that our true reality is love, and that the perceptual world in which we live is a dream filled with nightmarish fantasies of guilt, sin, attack, and defense.

As we make the choice to lift ourselves up from the perceptual world and live in the world of God's love, "thank you" becomes a way of life. As we become aware of God's gifts of eternal love and peace, the words "thank you" are increasingly the only ones on our lips.

We can learn to say "thank you" for the day whether it is stormy or sunny. I used to curse when it rained, because then I could not play tennis. I was concerned only with "getting." The possibility that I had been given an opportunity to be grateful and to give love to others was certainly not in my consciousness.

The ego is quick to say that it is absolutely ridiculous to say "thank you" if you have lost your job, your house, or your most cherished relationship. The ego would further say that if everything happening to us is supposed to be positive and a lesson from God, then we don't need the lesson or God.

However, the teacher who resides in our hearts would say that everything that happens in the perceptual world is but a new opportunity to choose the belief system of love, of God, a world where there is no form but only love.

Imagine what the world would be if the only words we spoke, to God and to one another, were "Thank you!" Each time we express our gratitude by extending our love to all, there is a little more light in the world, and a little less darkness.

We can learn to retrain our minds to count our blessings rather than our misfortunes. By surrendering to love, by surrendering to God, we can go through each day acknowledging one another with love and gratitude.

How quickly our world changes as we learn to return

all the love that is continuously given to us by our Source. What greater gratitude can we give to our Creator than choosing to love one another unconditionally by seeing the face of God in everyone.

I am grateful beyond words for all the people who have come into my life to be my teachers. There were many times I did not consider them my teachers. On the contrary, I saw them as my enemies in the same way I saw God as my enemy.

What a relief it is to know at last that everyone is my friend. How liberating to know that the only enemies I've ever had were the conflicting thoughts of my ego.

Therefore I say to all, with all my heart:

> Thank you for the lesson in forgiveness.
> Thank you for the lesson in patience.
> Thank you for the lesson in gentleness.
> Thank you for the lesson in love
> In peace
> And in happiness.

> "Love is the way I walk in gratitude."
> —*A Course in Miracles*

EPILOGUE

Writing this book has been wonderful therapy for me. Things have come up that I didn't realize I was still holding on to. In the process, I was reminded once again that I cannot rid myself of any internal darkness and find peace of mind until I am willing to bring that darkness into my conscious awareness.

I still go through periods when I resist believing that there is a journey I need to take, when I believe I am already home in the heart of God. Not a day goes by when I am not tempted to judge and condemn another person or myself.

And yet, increasingly, my intention is to make each day a living prayer. I am finding more consistency in asking myself the simple question, in every interchange: "What is this communication achieving? Is it for joining with others and with God, or is it for creating separation?"

I am finding that to go out of darkness into light, I have only to be a little more kind, a little more gentle and loving to those around me, and to myself. It has been in showing love to myself that I have had the greatest difficulty.

The simplicity of choosing to live a life of love, rather than a life of fear, is more clearly becoming a reality for me. The power of simply remembering God, and remembering that my true identity is love, has been beyond anything I could have imagined.

I thank you, dear reader, for being with me through the pages of this book. I invite you to join with me in recognizing that each of us does indeed make a difference. Let us all join in love, and know that in sharing the thoughts of love and peace with one another we bring the miracle of light into the world.

We can have a world where darkness is no longer found, where there is no pain or suffering, and where love is the answer to all things.

Let us help one another remember that we cannot do it all by ourselves. Let us join together to demonstrate in every area of our lives, that:

Whatever the question is, love is the answer.
Whatever the problem is, love is the answer.
Whatever the fear is, love is the answer.
Whatever the illness is, love is the answer.
Whatever the pain is, love is the answer.
Love is the answer no matter what
Because love is all there is.